Seven Stories
To Light the Way Home

BOOK THREE
of the *Greater Reality* Series

Cynthia Spring and Frances Vaughan

Wisdom Circles Publishing

Wisdom Circles Publishing
www.cindyspring.com
cspring@cindyspring.com

Cover graphic: Image of the Pleiades @Mironovfoto/*depositphotos.com*

Typesetting and Design: Margaret Copeland, Terragrafix
www.terragrafix.com

Publishing Consultant: Naomi Rose
www.naomirose.net

Proofreading: Gabriel Steinfeld
www.gabrielsteinfeld.com

Author photograph: Stu Selland

Story Seven: "Time to Go Home" included with permission
from Regina Ochoa.

BISAC: SEL032000 — SELF-HELP / Spiritual

Printed in the United States of America
First printing 2023

ISBN # 978-0-9996989-0-7

To Charlie, the man who taught me what love means.

— CYNTHIA SPRING

Contents

Story and Truth

 hen the world was still young, Truth walked around as naked as she was the day she was born. Whenever she came close to a village, people closed their doors and shut their windows, for everyone was afraid to face the Naked Truth. Understandably, Truth felt very alone and lonesome.

One day she encountered Story, who was surrounded by a flock of people of all ages who followed her everywhere she went. Truth asked her, "Why is it that people love you, but shy away from me?" Story, who was dressed in beautiful robes, advised Truth: "People love colorful clothes. I will lend you some of my robes and you will see that people will love you too." Truth followed her advice and dressed herself in the colorful robes of Story. It is said that from this day on, Truth and Story always walk together, and that people love both of them.

Dear Readers:

Welcome, dear readers. Welcome to *Seven Stories to Light the Way Home*, the third book in the Greater Reality series.

And welcome back if you've read Books One and Two of the Greater Reality trilogy (*Seven Questions About Life After Life*, and *Seven Questions About the Greater Reality*). The first two books—each formatted with Seven Questions—provided insights into Life After Life and the Greater Reality through the vantage point of Frances Vaughan, speaking to

Cynthia Spring "from the balcony" after her death. This book continues the "seven" motif, containing Seven Stories. Each story is like a puzzle piece. Pick one up and it's interesting in its own right. Yet put them together and a whole picture starts to emerge.

Imagine a starry night sky, sparkling with the great expanse of our galaxy. Imagine that each star offers a threshold, or a portal, into something we're calling "The Greater Reality." How many portals are there? Too many to count. This book offers seven of them. If you peek at the Greater Reality through each of these portals, you can put together an expansive view of your own making.

This book is about expanding your consciousness by creating new ways to understand how our human incarnation fits into a larger frame of existence that we all share, as well as new ways to experience it—new ways to discover that you already are very much a part of this larger existence.

We find ourselves living in a most challenging time. There's the threat of war, or actual war. Climate change is showing up in ways that no one can deny. A floating mass of seaweed twice as wide as the US continent. Countless numbers of species going extinct due to human carelessness or indifference. A pandemic killing millions of people worldwide. Now more than ever, we need stories to light the way home.

How Frances and I Came Together to Co-Create This Book

Frances Vaughan was a psychologist, psychotherapist, and author with an international following. She and I met through mutual friends in 2006. We started having dinners together, along with our husbands and a third couple, several times a year. That continued until September 2017, when Frances suddenly died of a heart complication.

In January 2018, I happened to attend a talk given by psychologist Matthew McKay. He described how devastated he had been by the loss of his 23-year-old son, Jordan, who had been murdered by robbers in 2008. Matthew eventually sought a way to connect with Jordan through automatic writing and was successful. He told this story in his book, *Seeking Jordan*, which contained segments of conversations he'd had with his son "from the other side." This inspired me to try to connect with Frances, using the same technique. I was successful on my first try. (A longer version of our story appears in Book One, *Seven Questions About Life After Life*.)

Stories Light the Way

Each of the seven stories in this book captures a moment, or an event, set in the context of a Greater Reality. The themes of Light and Community run throughout, although the stories are set in different times and places. The larger frame opens up through Frances' commentary and the dialogue between Frances and me, illuminating the broader meaning of the elements in each story.

Crossing thresholds greatly benefits from illumination. Story 1, *Deo Gratias*, offers Light for thresholds—those moments where we pass through a liminal space into a new reality. A threshold into new territory requires illumination to see what possibilities lie on the other side. A sixth-century Benedictine community provides the setting, and illumination comes in the form of a traveling minstrel seeking sanctuary.

Choicepoints need illumination. In Story 2, *The Roar of Angels*, fireman Frank Callahan has to make a choice that will greatly impact him as well as 400 first responders who perished with him in the 9-11 terrorist attack. On earth, they were a community in space/time; now they are bound together by their shared experience of death. Each person in that cohort had a critical choice to make about how to hold their experience. Illumination comes in the form of a wise elder. The choicepoint is about how to decide what matter more—revenge or forgivenss.

Co-creation needs illumination. Story 3, *Harps in the Trees,* is a delightful tale that illuminates the dance of co-creation. Recognizing that there are connections that weave through space and time gives us a much richer sense of how our own life evolves, along with everything around us. It also illustrates how difficult it is to give credit to any one factor in a creative endeavor. This story expands our sense of community. An ancient forest in Scotland provides the setting. Illumination comes in the form of a harpist and her wooden harp.

Communication with the other side needs illumination. In Story 4, *Love Calls,* we learn that we can communicate with loved ones who have left their bodies and now exist as conscious beings in a Greater Reality. We see that much comfort could be available for those consumed by grief if they knew (as millions of people have discovered) not only that such communication is possible, but that those on the other side long for it too. A community of people who have lost sons or daughters has sprung up to offer such connections.

Staying on track with our life purpose needs illumination. Story 5, *Homeless People Welcome,* is based on how each of us is born into our incarnation with a purpose that we've chosen for that lifetime. Sometimes we need illumination to help that choice stay on track. *Homeless People Welcome* tells us a tale of two people whose lives intersect at a health clinic during the time of COVID—members of a larger community of Black and Brown people sharing the reality of a pandemic. The two men provide illumination for each other.

Keeping hope alive in situations of daily, even desperate, challenge needs illumination. Story 6, *Starving Children Don't Cry,* illuminates how when the going gets really tough and the challenge to stay the course becomes a day-to-day struggle, events can happen on a daily basis to light the way. Ingrid, a volunteer in a Jordanian refugee camp, draws strength from the people she serves, a community of 80,000 people.

Finding our way back to our soul group needs illumination. In Story 7, *Time to Go Home,* we are introduced to the most important Light experience of all: finding our way back to our soul group as we leave our body behind. This exquisite story was given to us by a person who witnessed and guided her dear friend to the other side as the friend lay dying in a hospice. It weaves together strands of illumination from the earlier books in the Greater Reality Series. And Frances appears in the story as well.

These seven stories capture and expand upon all the themes and principles found in Books One and Two. We hope you enjoy them and find these messages and insights illuminating for your own journey, and those times when you have to decide what matters now.

Commentary from Frances

After each story, Frances provides us with her wisdom to reveal how that story connects to the themes of the Greater Reality trilogy. She and I also dialogue about lessons to be learned. Here's what Frances has to say about Book Three, in response to my request that she add her insights to this introduction:

Frances: See the [Greater Reality] trilogy as a course in the Greater Reality of existence. There will be something for you that will spark the divine wisdom that is in all of us. You can kindle that spark and lead some on a journey of learning — an emergent and diverse community that models a new way of being. Many other people are doing the same. You can be one who does not fear disaster, knows that death is a transition. You can communicate with people on "the other side," and know that this lifetime is only one lifetime. Those are our principles, our Greater Reality teachings.

The challenge is to let go of the strict attachment to a space/time reality, and discover how it meshes with the larger framework of the Greater Reality — very difficult to do without effort. But now there are many people — writers, poets, and musicians among others — who offer us a roadmap through the phenomenal world of interacting objects and cause-and-effect events, and see it for what it is: a movie. [We described this more fully in Book Two.] It's a compelling movie, a movie that can move heart and soul with joy or unbearable tragedy. But [you can learn] to straddle both worlds — the earthbound unfolding story of your life as you're living it, and the expanded consciousness that you are, watching it unfold in ways that serve your purpose and ways that don't. What you want, ideally, is for your expanded consciousness to inform your life, and for your life to expand your consciousness beyond what you came into your current incarnation with.

Now, in Book Three, we will make this clearer and show how "listening to the music of the harps" is a beautiful and necessary part of the demise of the unsustainable situation on earth now [climate change, COVID, political unrest, exploitation of Earth's resources etc.]. Please remember [if you read Books One and Two] what I have said about the necessary and inescapable cataclysms that accompany change.

Cynthia: What can we say to those who are holding out hope and say we must not give in to despair? To those who say a new age is possible?

Frances: It is possible. A new and more balanced period will come. What you and our readers, and those who know that more upheavals are coming, are doing is ALL TO THE GOOD. Nothing is lost. But much is transformed into higher frequencies.

It is not for you to sort out which future scenario will prevail. None of you will be incarnate as you are now. Those of us who are offering insights into your future are only trying to spare you some pain, some grief, some wasted effort in trying to fashion a better world from the detritus of the current one. Visionaries see "a promised land." You are a visionary. The promised land is not within the grasp of current inhabitants of Earth. It is across the bridge, "on the other side."

Cynthia: And I want to emphasize your words, "IT'S ALL TO THE GOOD." Anything that each one of us contributes during these times to love, community, compassion and mutual support is planting the seeds for a future world that works for everyone.

How to Read This Book

Please consider each story on its own merits. After reading each one, what can you add to Frances' commentary that you can use as guidance for yourself? Each reader adds to the co-creation of this book by reading it, interpreting it personally and individually, and sharing the expanded understanding with others.

Deo Gratias

The Light at the Threshold

≈℮

Scene: *Midnight in central Italy... the sixth century CE, after the fall of the Western Roman Empire and the beginning of what's known as the Dark Ages. After a long period of decline, the final ransacking of Rome by invaders took place in 476 CE. Travel had since become treacherous. No longer were the Roman legions patrolling the roadways. The Pax Romana of earlier centuries had devolved into many small wars fought by a variety of tribes. Dense forests filled areas that didn't have towns. By 500 CE, one could no longer depend on a semblance of law and order.*

This is one traveler's story.

hank God the rainstorm had passed. But the cold wind was still unrelenting. The traveler, a minstrel, had been more than eager to reach the monastery after spending three nights sleeping on the cold forest floor, aware of predators in the vicinity both human and feral. And he had a message, a vital message, to impart to the monks.

Now, knowing he would be received at this Benedictine monastery with food and a safe place to rest like all travelers, he knocked on the monastery's wooden gate—once, then again. With relief, he heard the familiar response offered to travelers at all such monasteries: "*Deo gratias,*" the porter shouted. "Thanks be to God that you have come."

The porter stood on the threshold between two worlds—the world the traveler needed sanctuary from, and the hushed, sacred world within the monastery walls. "*Deo gratias,* Brother," the traveler said, answering the porter's greeting with his own. "It is good to be with you."

This monastery had been founded by Saint Benedict himself. He wrote out his Rule Book for this monastery, and then others sprang up, filled with young and not-so-young men who wanted to devote themselves to Christianity and have some stability in their lives. Over a dozen small monasteries had been founded in central and southern Italy. They formed a loose federation, each one having its own abbot to decide how Benedict's rules should apply. They recognized their brotherhood by allowing monks to travel freely among them, always expecting to be greeted with Benedict's mandated hospitality. Extending that hospitality to strangers was a founding principle.

The greeting of "Deo gratias" had several meanings. One was thankfulness that the visitor had survived the terrors of the forest. A more important message was also conveyed: "We welcome you because you are a messenger. You may tell us what is transpiring in other parts of the Italian states and beyond. More than that, you may have come to stretch our minds and souls, to prod us out of our complacency."

Lighting the way with his candle, the porter led the visitor past the vegetable gardens and into the monastery's inner courtyard. Even with the dim outlines allowed by the dark, the traveler could see the covered colonnade of the cloister where the monks would go to read and pray. And nearby had to be a *scriptorium*, where the monks stored and wrote or copied written scrolls by hand, sometimes illustrating them. Monasteries, the traveler knew well, were the central storehouses of knowledge.

Once they were inside the sprawling residence that served to house several dozen monks, the porter woke the cook and asked that a meal be prepared for the itinerant minstrel. The traveler sat at a wooden table and gratefully ate the simple fare. After that kindness, he was led to the guest quarters and given a small room to sleep in, complete with bed, nightshirt and water basin. Then the porter bid the visitor good night.

The next night, all the monks took respite from their day of work and prayer, and gathered in the dining hall to listen with rapt attention to the stories told by the visitor. Being cloistered in a monastery with no outside communication for months meant that they had no sense of the greater reality of political and social events outside the monastery walls. There also was the possibility that the visitor had news that was important to the monastery's survival.

This particular visit offered something even more rare than simply news: the wandering minstrel entertained the monks with songs of heroism, and lyrics from the *Odyssey* describing the founding of Rome by the Trojans. But when he had brought his songs to a close, this minstrel offered prophecy as well.

"Listen closely," he advised them, his eyes settling first on one of the monks, then another and another, until the entire gathering felt the intensity of what he was about to tell. As one, they fell silent.

"All the literature that has been gained through the centuries of Roman rule is at risk of being lost forever. Books must be preserved."

The monks, so accustomed to silence, let their silence speak.

"The precious scrolls with messages of the evangelists of Christianity are in jeopardy," the traveler said urgently. "You must make more copies of these scrolls, and hide them in secure places."

The minstrel reminded them that Jesus had taught a moral code promising everlasting life to those who followed it. The Gospels offered answers to the great questions of human existence: *Why are we born? What is our responsibility in relationships? What is the path of the saintly person?*

The message was clear: "*This wisdom must not be lost. The monastery must hold the Light. It must not fall into the chaos and strife that is overtaking Western Europe.*"

The monks were amazed and humbled by their new mission.

Commentary

Cynthia: What are the lessons we can learn from this story?

Frances: Hospitality is not only a kind and generous way to treat a guest. It is a two-way street when it's done well. It is a gathering of friends, as we used to do as a sixsome. There was a level of hospitality by the host couple. But at the best of gatherings, there was an exchange of wisdom, of heartspace, and mutual support.

This is the quality of *Comitas*—community as an essential piece of what's needed to mend and heal the divisions among the humans these days. When, and if, it's possible to reconvene in gatherings—circles, dinners, potlucks, support groups, singing groups, quilting groups, sports watching, all manner of gatherings where people put aside their politics, their religious differences, and all manner of prejudices and get to know each other across boundaries, in neighborhoods and civic centers—these gatherings will begin the healing and [they will] strengthen the fabric of the whole.

C: That's beautiful, Frances.

F: Yes, and necessary. The time for confrontations over differences is over—at least for now. What leaders should be encouraging is gatherings of love and sharing, and getting to know each other. The angry mob has shown itself to be destructive, not constructive. A peaceful protest can be a form of community.

C: Sometimes those two forms get tangled up. What else is to be learned from this story?

F: The comparison of the post-Roman empire, at least the western part based in Rome, with what could be the fate of the post-American empire is clear: chaos, danger, the need for oases of hospitality for strengthening the bonds, for preserving the wisdom and stories of the past.

C: There is so much implied in that story and you have brought it to light. Can you tell us one more lesson to be discovered from *Deo Gratias*?

F: There are many more. But another one has to do with what it means to be in the company of others, as with the monks in the story. They love and support each other, each in his own unique way. And it's not all sweetness and co-creation. That's why Benedict came up with his Rule Book. Humans are imperfect beings, needing guidelines for behaviors and norms, for the ways differences are handled.

Problems arise when the "rules" do not succor the person, fill his needs, but constrain him. Rules need to be flexible, which is why Benedict said each head abbot of a monastery can interpret them as appropriate to the situation. And you hope that the head abbot is the most enlightened or saintly in the group. But that's not always so. Another lesson to be learned by the group! The give-and-take of making groups work well is an art form. The Quakers are one lineage who do it fairly well.

Human beings and all of creation are a constantly evolving wholistic mass of people, plants, other animals, locales too. A forest or a small town, or a mountain top, do not stay static. Nothing does. So one of the purposes of creating those groupings I spoke of is to keep checking on what's working and what's not working in the matrix of the tribe.

C: What a treasure trove of insights from one short story.

F: I'm sure there's more, but that is plenty for an opening session on expanding and exploring the messages contained.

C: *Deo gratias* is, of course, the Latin for "Thanks be to God." I think we should review our use of that word—God—for the sake of readers who have not read Book One. That word has carried so many layers of meaning throughout the centuries. It also carries much baggage too, in terms of how it's used as a cudgel to beat nonbelievers into submission, or claim superiority—as in "God is on my side."

The way we've used the term God in this trilogy is as a way to capture an Omnipresence, a sense of All That Is. Belief in a singular external God figure is still very strong in America. I was watching a news program where the mother of one of the many young Black men killed recently by a policeman was being interviewed. She was asked how she's able to carry on her crusade to stop police brutality, because she tries to support other families who have lost a child to violence, and that always brings up her own loss. Her answer was simple: "I pray to God for strength." I wondered how I would speak to her and share what you and I feel is a more expansive and inclusive experience of God?

F: First of all, you recognize that for the mother of Eric Garner, this *is* a God in whatever ways she configures and experiences it. *It is her reality.* You cannot say it doesn't exist. For her, it does. She is creating her own reality and as we know, co-creating it with many others.

C: I see what you're saying. But aren't we putting forth a broader, more inclusive version of a divine presence, an Omnipresence of Light and Love, that includes us as well— not one separate from an external figure?

F: Yes indeed, we are. [That's] because it works for us. It has more explanatory power, which is how scientists describe the process. When one hypothesis supersedes another, it explains better our direct experience. Einstein's relativity theory had more power to create new ways of manipulating and changing the reality of humans. Space travel was one result. But then quantum physics came along to supersede and include relativity theory. And quantum theory has given us a much greater understanding of reality, including nonlocal consciousness—a bigger frame.

And therein lies the clue. Plain old Newtonian physics works very well in many situations humans find themselves in, like building a house. No need for quantum physics there.

So too, for [Eric Garner's mother]. Her reliance on God works very well for her in the terrible loss of her son. She doesn't need to invoke anything more "cosmic" than that. Her story is as "alive" as our story. Her God is not dead. She and millions of others are keeping Him (it's usually a Him) alive and well. The emphasis is on "our" stories, which should be inclusive. They show the way to a larger understanding of reality. But they do not discard old forms that work very well for people. To open a can, a can opener will do nicely. You don't need a Mars lander.

C: That's it. That's the kind of answer I was looking for. I must carefully create an explanation of the Greater Reality that includes a God when God the can opener is a very adequate tool. But in situations like we're in now—with upheavals threatening to make humans extinct—we need a larger sense of how we all fit together in a harmonious All That Is. Into a sense of One. That is the shift we need to make.

Will this COVID pandemic be enough to wake us up— to change course? To revision the world we live in?

F: Perhaps, for some. But many will have to give up their lives, as in all great transitions, for that to happen. You will be one of them.

C: I hope I do it well.

F: You will.

C: So, is part of the message of Book Three: Be prepared to give up your life, your "human experience," your incarnation?

F: I'm afraid so. There are many metaphors available—doing it for the children, for the seventh generation, planting a seed for a tree you will never sit under. We'll find them all. This is a call to arms. But not weapons—with arms of Love, arms with which to embrace each other. Arms pointing to a greater reality that we all share. This is our opportunity to have many realize that this singular life is more like a part in a play, a co-creation that has many possible outcomes, each one valid as a learning experience.

I see a world cascading into oblivion. A world that could no longer withstand the onslaught of the human species.

Earth has reached a tipping point—over she goes—into an abyss of falling, falling into a new form—unrecognizable to those who have known and still cherish the madness— the crowds, the advance of technologies stunning and inhuman in their power to change a plant-based world into one of zeroes and ones. With no balance, no respect for all the other living creatures for whom zeroes and ones are meaningless and always will be.

C: What can those of us do to ride out the chaos?

F: Hold all as dear, all as precious. Hold the world that is shuddering and crying and opening to depths of love it has never known. A new consciousness is being birthed. Many will want to return to the old ways. Many will try. But now those ways will seem awkward and anachronistic. Just as the "New Age" ways have seemed out of synch with the consensus reality, but will now help define "the new normal."

C: I hope so. I sense there will be a lot more dislocation before the love and community and innovation of new forms establish themselves and come to define what matters. It will take a while.

F: Yes it will. And people who have died in order to show us the way will rejoice in their heavens, in their homes in the Greater Reality. *Deo gratias* is also a greeting heard by some as they cross the bridge to the other side.

C: In this opening story, the scene is set in the "Dark Ages" of Earth's history. That term is used by some historians to describe a period of economic, political, and cultural stagnation. In *Deo Gratias*, a stranger comes a long with a message for the monks to "preserve the literature." What "strange" sources should *we* look toward for guidance?

F: Everything from the family cookbook to stories of visitations from UFOs. The cookbook that provides tried-and-true recipes handed down from generation to generation stores more than ingredients for a dish. You can count on those dishes to please the people you hold as family. Look at what that means in a broader frame. The amount of each ingredient, the way to cook the meal, all point to a wisdom of harmony—what goes together and forms the foundation for family cohesiveness.

Beyond that, the same principles apply to our neighborhoods, villages, towns. However, as we've pointed out so many times in Books One and Two, old ways of being in harmony sometimes don't work anymore—ways that don't produce harmony but instead, produce chaos. Ways that isolate some and disenfranchise some and not others. Ways that disrespect the bounty and resources of Mother Earth and damage Her ability to provide sustenance.

All of those "old ways," which someday may come to be called our *Dark Age*, are being re-examined and found faulty by many from different vantage points. Whether the forces envisioning harmony and the creation of sustainable forms will be enough, and "in time," remains to be seen.

Are we ready to cross the threshold and engage whatever is before us? What gives us the strength to move forward with today: with assurance calling out that loving welcome, Deo Gratias, to a future that is unsure, unknown?

—ESTHER DE WAAL, author, *To Pause at the Threshold*

The Roar of Angels

The Light at a Choicepoint

~✎

Frank Callahan (1950-2001) was a New York City fire captain who, along with others on his team, perished in the line of duty during the 9/11 attacks. The following quote is from Jeanne Love, the person who channeled Frank's message to the world:

"As we got closer to the 5-year anniversary of September 11, 2001, 'Frank' came through with this communication. As Frank dictated his story, I couldn't help but experience a deep emotional connection to what he was sharing. I basically cried through the whole writing. I think this Message serves as a powerful reminder for us all as to how we can approach the darkness and how it can change."

~✎

Scene: *It's September 11, 2001, in New York City. A jumbo jet loaded with passengers crashes into a World Trade Center tower. Fire, Death, Destruction are everywhere. An accident? Twenty minutes later a second passenger jet filled with human beings crashes into the second tower. Infernos rage inside both towers.*

These are not accidents. These are deliberate acts of terrorism. Over four hundred first responders die trying to rescue the people trapped in the buildings before the structures collapse. For several thousand inside, it's too late.

Fire Captain Frank Callahan is present, representing many who died and lost their families. He is here to tell us the story of what happened after he died. We learn about the power of the millions of prayers sent on 9/11.

This story has been derived from the original message channeled by medium Jeanne Love in 2006, with her permission.

rank: I am happy to say that many of us have found our new lives and found our peace. Many still linger in resentment and choose to live in the darkness that 9/11 created for all of us as Americans. But many more have made other choices.

Some have decided to grow in their spirits, to recognize that we have far more power to change things than any of us would have ever imagined pre-9/11. Some of us have stayed closer to our families than we ever thought possible. Some have chosen simply to move on and walk away from that day and the lives they once knew. And so we have processed these experiences individually. I come as the representative of those of us who died, to warn, but also assure—to paint a new picture and to call for the understanding that is necessary to change the grief into Light-Action.

Frank tells us that one of the first things that brought together those who died in the tragedy was the incredible roar of thousands of angels singing.

Frank: We almost forgot who we were and where we had come from because the roar of the angels' music completely surrounded us. We had been drawn collectively into this huge hall and were promptly held by thousands of lighted beings. We could never have imagined anything so beautiful.

When I "came to," so to speak, and realized what was happening, I asked a kindly gentleman sitting next to me who all these people/beings were, and how was it that the music was so beautiful? He responded in a way I will never forget. He took my hands and said, as he looked into my eyes, "Son...this is the result of the world praying for you."

I cried. I cried deeply and reverently because I had NEVER known such kindness. I cried because I knew my family and the families and friends of the others who were lost would be crying in desperation and grief. I cried because I felt sorry for those "on the ground" who didn't know this.

※

Frank tells us that he looked over to see where his "boys" were, the ones who had died in the attack with him. He wanted to make sure that everyone "got out" and had come over here—wherever "here" was. Then the stranger took his hand and pointed at the horizon....

※

Frank: I couldn't believe my eyes. There was this beautiful magnificent eagle flying all around us. Somehow it seemed larger than the biggest commercial jets. It was proud as it flew but it was more than a beautiful bird. It had several foreign-looking fellows in its talons. At first I didn't recognize them, but I started to shake as I recognized that these foreign fellows must be the hijackers of the planes that ran into the towers.

I was appalled and angry. The others grew anxious as they recognized who these men were. The anger started to catch hold like a fire that couldn't be stopped. All of a sudden the beautiful angelic voices stopped and we found ourselves in a horrible place, full of anxiety and torment. We could barely breathe. How could this be, and where had we gone? The gentleman, thankfully, was still holding my hand and reassuring me that this moment could be temporary. At this point I didn't understand anything that was happening. All I knew was that I seemed be in the darkness again. The pain, the smothering heat, the screams of death were everywhere now. I begged my friend for help and to get me and the others out of this place. "Show me the way," I screamed. "Show me the way out!" Nothing happened and I was angry and felt betrayed. Was I to burn in hell for this? Was this hell? What was happening? From the most beautiful place to the darkest abyss, all in a few seconds. Was this where we were doomed to stay, in this pit of ugliness?

I looked around and realized that there were many suffering close by me. We tried to talk to each other about what was taking place but it was to no avail. We were lost, destined to wander in the atrocity of this attack, labeled by the very act of being connected to the rescue attempts we were trying to make. What was happening?

Then the man took me gently aside and said, "This is the other side of prayer. The words of success at destroying others have shaped this event and experience. Those who wanted this destruction are rejoicing and this is the energy that is surrounding you now." Oh, my God, I couldn't believe this sudden shift. Were we all destined to be locked into these prayers of destruction and seeming payback by those radicals who shaped these terrible events?

Then this kindest of men looked at me again in the eye and charged me with this question: "Which do you choose?"

"What do you mean, which do I choose? I HAVE a choice?"

"Yes, thankfully, you do. Do you wish to be saved and healed by the choir of angels sent to you in prayer by those who believe in the power of love and forgiveness, or do you wish to swim in the sea of despair and retribution?"

You would think that I could answer easily and quickly, but the experience was so foreign to me and so distant from any experiences on earth that I simply had to take some time to let it all sink in. My friend continued to stand with me and said, "If you go to the light, your family of co-workers will go with you too. You are greatly respected and show such courage in the face of danger. They trust you to know. You have the power to shift this experience and bring truth and joy in the midst of deep despair."

Frank realized in that moment that he had the opportunity to continue to lead his trusting men back into the thoughts and prayers streaming like rivers into the hall of angels. He sensed that the hellish pain of anger and retribution they were experiencing would quickly be removed. Frank squeezed his new friend's hand, indicating that it was the release of darkness he wished for himself and his men.

Frank: Then the stranger asked me the most difficult question ANYONE could ever ask me: "Do you see the eagle again?"

"Yes," I replied.

"Do you see the men still in the talons of the eagle?"

"Yes," I replied again.

He continued: "In order to get back to the prayer, the light, the forgiveness, the healing you so desperately need, you must forgive those men . . . those men who took your life, their own, and thousands of others."

I thought I would die all over again as the anger and resentment began to build inside of me. How COULD he ask that of me? But he just continued to hold my hand and smile, sending me warm thoughts of comfort and clarity.

All of a sudden I saw my grandma and my aunties. They were standing all together, holding each other and smiling. I didn't hear them speak but I heard their hearts singing to me. They sang to me songs of the God of Love and forgiveness that we used to sing at church. They reminded me that the only way to God was to forgive. I began to cry uncontrollably as I recognized what this all meant: I could not move into the place of Heaven while carrying discontent, anguish, hatred, and despair. The angels sang to us as a result of all those people around the world praying for us. These prayers were so beautiful, so forgiving, that nothing could keep us from the joy of God.

When the hijackers were first brought to us by the eagle, my own darkness had undermined the beauty of the prayers we were receiving. In essence we were giving the prayers away, denying their power. Our own anger was betraying us, and nothing would save us from that darkness as long as we were honoring and reinforcing our own anguish and hatred.

In those few moments as the men and I were coming to grips with this, the sounds of the angels started to reach our sad ears once again.

～◎

It took a while for his men to come to the same conclusions that Frank had. But once they did, the Light grew brighter, their senses grew keener and their hearts started to feel lifted. Their tears were now for this revelation, this choice point of which path to follow ... and their grief for those who did not know this and for the pain they would carry needlessly.

＊

Frank: I am now working towards peace in our world. I have worked tirelessly to understand how this whole thing works. I have tried to communicate with my family and friends and have had some success, but the grief keeps them from knowing the joy that we are all "right here"—just on different sides of the light.

[I hold deep gratitude] to everyone who has prayed and done rescue work for those of us who left our physical bodies during the attack on the towers. I don't choose to see the tower attacks as darkness. I choose to see them as light events: a time when we were shown how important it is to choose what we will serve: the consciousness of love and forgiveness, or the painful memories of loss and destruction. You all need to know how powerful prayer is, and continues to be, for all of us.

Commentary

Cynthia: Frances, please share with us your insights on Frank's story.

Frances: Frank Callahan is a good man who gave his life trying to save others. That is always a noble story. We recognize the divine aspect of that kind of story—even when we don't mention it. We recognize ourselves in the "other." We are saving ourselves. Or trying to. Whether we save a person from death—for instance, in an accident or suicide—does not matter as much as the act of saving. That is the lesson. The more compassion we muster, the more the saving of other beings becomes the norm and not the exception, the more Light there is to show the way.

Frank spoke of a deafening roar. He heard it as sound, instead of seeing it as Light. No matter. Light is only one way to describe God's presence—the presence of the Whole—the I AM. When a soul recognizes itself as I am the I AM, it becomes united with the All There Is.

Frank experiences the I AM in the Hall of Angels. His anger, confusion, and whatever else was still present from his 9-11 experience was drowned out by the roar of angels. What he and the men he cherished—his fellow firemen, who knew they were each committed to a life-or-death struggle in going into the crumbling World Trade Center buildings—it didn't matter. What mattered was the commitment, the unity of purpose, the final act of a life well-lived for each of them.

And give their lives they did. But Frank tells us that they entered a hall filled with joy, with enormous welcome, a much grander vision of the Benedictine monastery [in Story 1] but equal in its intention: You are home. You are safe. You will be taken care of here.

But then we find out there's a catch. Your soul must vibrate at the same frequency as all the prayers coming from millions of incarnates holding you in their prayers.

And you see the perpetrators in the eagle's talons. How can you possibly forgive them after knowing all the pain they caused? And in an instant you learn that the Earth's moral code is not the same as Heaven's compassion. A moral code may be useful at this stage of human development. But not as punishment or revenge. Individuals who cause harm must be prevented from doing more harm.

But the landscape of Heaven is spacious and is tended only by loving individuals whose commitment is to all of the souls, not just the "good" ones. We want the so-called terrorists to recognize they are divine too. To know they are not separate from the beloved community. Going through a life review and directly experiencing the pain they have caused will be part of their entry. But not as punishment. More like touching a hot burner on a stove. It hurts too much. [They say] "That's not something I want to experience again. I would rather serve my people's needs as a caregiver, not as a weapon for vengeance or power."

C: But as we've said in Books One and Two, there are souls who must go through some "rehab," must be woken up to remember all of this "extravaganza."

F: They will learn. It may take more lifetimes. They will learn. They always do, and we will aid them in their journey because they are us—parts of ourselves that have lost the way—temporarily. When you can see the other as part of yourself, it will all happen quickly.

Frank has a choicepoint. He tells the story with excruciating honesty. He didn't know if he could choose forgiveness.

The stranger's pointing to the confusion of Frank's men, how they were depending on his leadership, made it not simply an individual decision [on Frank's part] but yet again an act of great wisdom and compassion.

Not all the souls who had crossed over with him followed him back to the Hall of Angels. But you can be sure that Frank continues to serve those who stayed behind, and to let them know they are always welcome to join the others in the Light.

It is interesting that in the stories where someone has crossed over suddenly, the person wants the grieving ones on earth to know: "I'm OK. I'm fine. We'll see each other again." We hear that story tens of thousands of times. The grief is much more about the living person's loss than the dead person's experience, although it can be both. That's fine. Grief teaches us about the depth of Love. Pain and grief can be fine teachers of Joy and Love. It's all part of the curriculum of an Earth incarnation.

C: Can you say something about Frank's seeing his relatives during his choicepoint moment?

F: Ah yes. His grandmother and aunties, as he calls them, are there—relatives always come as escorts and helpers. They remind him of the Christian lessons of forgiveness—authentic forgiveness that is buried deep in the authentic message of Jesus. It also helped Frank make the choice to go to the Light.

Here there is no punishment per se, just separation from the Whole. Those who chose to not go with Frank, to not forgive but to hold onto their anger, are a part of it. But they isolate themselves outside of it *as they see it*. They need healing—becoming whole again—not punishment. They need Love. Earth is a bruising place. We all need Love and TLC [tender loving care] to become Whole after the rough situation that some have been in. That will happen. *Remember, here there is no punishing, only healing.*

I am the Air I breathe.
I am the Ground I walk.
I am the Voice I hear.
I am the Song I sing.

I AM the I AM
I am Love.

I am the Wind in the Universe.
I am the Stars in the Cosmos.
I am the Creator of Thoughts.
I am These Thoughts.

I am Love.
I AM the I AM

— From poem by Frances Vaughan

Harps in the Trees

The Light of Co-Creation

~◎~

Scene: *A fog swirls and a light wind is blowing. We enter a young forest taking root in what someday will be called the Scottish Highlands. Wind through the tree leaves was the first music the young trees heard. Different varieties of trees—oak, ash, spruce, sycamore—are listening. And they answer. Their leaves and limbs produce a variety of sounds as the winds pass by. It's a simple but beautiful melody. Birds come, adding lyrics to the music.*

Now we are in the same forest eons later in the sixth century, and we see a monk sitting at the base of one tree. He is composing music for voices and harps, to be played at sacred festivals. The trees listen to the monk chanting his creation, and they are enchanted. The music of harps is a link between heaven and earth. The Trees have never heard music so beautiful. How can they add to these soul-stirring sounds? This is their story.

he Trees in the Scottish forest feel there is music alive inside them. They have more emotion to express than even the Wind can orchestrate. The Trees want to sing. To do that they must extend themselves to invite a co-creation. How? The elements contribute. The Sun strengthens the fibers of the wood. The Water soaks the roots, providing stability to withstand strong winds. And the Earth makes sure the Trees receive nutrients from neighboring plants and fungi. Trees exhale, animals inhale. Animals exhale, Trees inhale.

Planting seeds in people's dreams is another way the Trees get around. They whisper: "Imagine harps made by master instrument builders who love birthing the harps from the wood of the trees. This area will become known for the creation of such harps."

The idea catches on, and soon the town of Strathpeffer is known for its fine harp makers and melodious harps. The harp makers, the harp players, the lumberjacks, and a village to support them—all working together to free the harps that lie dormant in the wood. The spirit of the Trees has found resonance with the spirit of the humans.

Now in a city named for St. Francis of Assisi, there lives a harpist, known the world over. She composes, plays and teaches the music she knows and loves. Her name is Adaira. One night she has a vivid dream. She is standing in a gray, swirling mist on the edge of a dark forest. She is dressed in a monk's hooded cloak, holding a lighted taper. A group of monks are walking behind her, also holding tapers to light the way.

The next day, Adaira receives an invitation to perform and teach at a harp festival in Scotland. She accepts, and plans to bring some of her students. And what a coincidence! These students have harps that came from a Highlands forest in the north. So the plan is to play at the festival, then journey to the forest in Strathpeffer to serenade the Trees with harp music. The harps would come Home.

All came to pass. Nestled in the Trees, the harpists played the music the Trees had longed to hear for millennia. Played upon the fibers of their ancestors, by people who had come to express their gratitude. Oh Joyous Day!

The next day, Adaira went to the forest for a solo performance. She found a perfect fallen log and began to play the music she had chosen. But it wasn't flowing the way she had planned. Something wasn't right. The music sounded dull. Even the weather was unsettled. This was the perfect setting for a person devoted to the harp made here. What did the Trees want?

She paused, cleared her mind, took a deep breath and began again. A medieval melody was pouring out from her fingers on the strings. She didn't recognize it, although she knew many compositions from that era. As she continued playing, a luminescence began to emerge from the Trees and surround the grove.

Everyone present saw it, felt it. Something or someone was playing through her, using her skill, her fingers, to create the music the Trees wanted to hear. When the music finished, she bowed deeply to the Trees in astonishment and gratitude.

Adaira was staying at the home of one of the harp makers. He was also a harpist and a scholar of ancient harp music. That evening she asked him if he knew any Gregorian chants from that area of Scotland. To her amazement, he began to play a Gregorian chant composed in dedication to St. Columba, a monk who became the patron saint of Scotland during the sixth century—the same music that had flowed through her fingers earlier that day. That was the piece the Trees wanted to hear. Maybe written by a monk in that very grove. Who knows?

The monks in Adaira's dream were centuries old, and in her dream she and her students were among them. They thought they had they come to honor the Trees. Did they have a resonant, timeless connection with the monks in medieval Scotland? Perhaps they were bidden not to simply visit, but also to complete a circle of creation begun by the Trees?

When did the music begin? In the winds and leaves of the early days? Where will it end? With the listeners of the music? Or will it ripple out into infinity?

The Highland Trees knew how to summon what they desired, using their understanding of co-creation, and then patiently waiting for their dream to manifest.

Commentary

Frances: What is the message of this beautiful story? So many. The Trees are enchanted by the music made by the wind passing through their limbs and leaves—music they are helping to co-create. They feel the rhythms of the Earth and know the songs they contain within their fibers.

The Trees have a beautiful existence in their forest in the Scottish Highlands. They are existing in a field of dreams. Dreams of becoming, transforming into other forms of being, tasting dimensions hinted at by monks and musicians who frequent these groves, who play instruments and who sing and chant melodies that come from the Source of all art and music and beauty—from the I AM.

Cynthia: Can you explain "I am the I AM" for readers who have not read Book Two?

F: It means we are divine.

C: What does *that* mean?

F: That we are co-creating all that we experience. That it's all evolving with each and every thought, kindness, and magnificent project or program or piece of music.

Right now during this pandemic on earth, so much is evolving through the heroic efforts of so many millions of people whose life trajectory brought them to this moment—to whatever place they find themselves—to provide care and comfort to all those who are ill and to those who are dying from the coronavirus. So many others who have found themselves to be "essential" during this time who never had considered themselves as such—in fact, quite the opposite. Receiving so much gratitude for doing simple things like being a cashier or a delivery person. It's an evolution in consciousness, and you can see it happening on a daily basis.

The Trees want to evolve just like the humans do. They want to serve their purpose of becoming incarnate as trees. They want to enjoy the limited and impermanent existence of life on earth and then move on into other forms on earth, and beyond.

Humans long to fulfill a purpose while incarnate and perpetuate themselves through their accomplishments, through their children, through their destiny as beings of Light and Love as all other beings do.

Even becoming a piece of paper, as this paper you are writing on now, fulfills a Tree's purpose. This contains the wisdom to be transmitted to others, and paper and pen is the medium for their expression. Again, when this becomes Book Three, you will turn this into a medium for others to learn from. Again on paper made from trees, or made from paper recycled from former paper, from trees.

C: As you speak, I'm experiencing the Dance of Co-Creation.... I see the plumeria blossom in Hawaii becoming the fragrance in my shampoo. I smell the coffee bean in Peru reaching my morning latte.

F: That's it! Being able to see that progression, every step of the way being a co-creation, is a way of understanding the lesson of incarnation. To move into material frequency, to participate in a myriad number of co-creations, and then to move on back into the greater reality with other co-creations to blend and adapt into more "life forms."

As we know, even the remnants of a "dead tree," one fallen in the forest, becomes a greenhouse of life forms for other species. Lichen, moss, mushrooms, nutrients of all kinds for the soil, the insects. Upright tree snags become storehouses for woodpeckers' acorns and hollows for small animals.

If you could see the fantastic number of offspring, of enterprises for other creatures going on in the short life of a tree, you could spend your life simply watching. And learning everything you need to know about life on earth without having to go to school.

Back to our trees in the forest that became harps in concert halls: yes, it is the desire, the evolutionary thrust, if you will—of a tree near Strathpefffen to become a harp. Just as some athletes want to excel in a professional sport, or as an artist craves a medium in order to express the Love and symmetry of Life, so too do certain trees have a harp in them. And those blessed harpmakers sense that yearning.

You can trace the journey as vibration to vibration— from the rustling of leaves to being played in a symphony, along with other instruments—violins, drums, brass horns—all co-created from elements of the planet and fashioned so that the vibration of the All That Is may be felt by those who are present.

Vibrations. We are each and all vibrations, frequencies of sound and light, that extend infinitely beyond human hearing range. When you see a particular tree destined to become a musical instrument, do you hear the harp? Like the psychic ability of clairvoyance or what's now called "remote viewing," humans are capable of "remote hearing"—being able to hear the sounds of the harp the tree's wood will produce. That skill is only available to a select few. It is available to many more who could activate remote hearing, as those who succeed at learning remote viewing do now.

C: So what you're saying is that gifted individuals could possibly stand near certain trees near Strathpeffen and hear the music of harps to come from the co-creation of tree and harp-maker? What is the lesson for those of us who may never cultivate "remote listening" in this lifetime?

F: That all is frequencies. That all is transitory. That all is change from one form to another. Trying to cling to one form of being, one step in your evolution—either as a co-creator or as a co-creation—is foolish. It cannot be done. Death of the body is a transition to another form of existence, just as the trees turn into harps and then into music. That is the lesson of Harps in the Trees. It is a beautiful one.

Every block of stone has a statue inside it and it is the task of the sculptor to discover it.... I saw the angel in the marble and carved until I set him free.

— MICHELANGELO

Love Calls

The Light through the Veil

༄

Scene: *Mary Ellen lies sleeping in the darkness, next to her husband, Rusty. A sound breaks the quiet, and she stirs in response. Is that the phone ringing in the middle of the night? Fogged with sleep, Mary Ellen thinks it might be; but since it only rings a couple of times, she turns over and goes back to sleep.*

Around 8 a.m. as the coffee is brewing, she checks the answering machine. There is a message. It is the police, asking her to please call them. She calls immediately and finds out that their teenage son Eugene died the day before, rock climbing in Yosemite with friends. He will not be coming home.

This is a story of after-death communication between a mother and son.

ene was an athlete. He could have excelled in many sports. But his commitment was to his schoolwork. He wanted an academic scholarship to college, not an athletic one, where one injury can end it all. The one physical activity he allowed himself was rock climbing. It was all the rage in his high school. A nearby movie theater that had been shut down for years was transformed into a rock-climbing emporium. It had easy, moderate, and difficult walls to practice on and master. Gene was proficient at all three levels.

Two nights after his fatal fall in Yosemite, Gene appeared in his parents' bedroom. Mary Ellen saw him clearly. Rusty didn't see or hear anything. This was Gene's message:

"Mom, I'm alive. I'm OK. I died and went to someplace better than heaven. Gramps is here. He met me as I crossed a bridge. I was pretty much in shock from the fall. My physical body must have been all broken up—but I was fine, intact, nothing broken, and Gramps was smiling at me with open arms. I'll be back when I get more situated here. I love you."

Mary Ellen was pretty sure this was some sort of grief hallucination on her part, especially since Rusty had seen and heard nothing. But it seemed very real, not just a dream. What could it be?

After Gene's funeral, Mary Ellen was in grief. She could hardly get out of bed. The tragedy had completely frozen the family's life. Gene was the oldest of three boys, the first-born who was going to lead the way.

Gene kept his promise. He returned many times—sometimes as an apparition, sometimes only as a felt presence, but always with messages of comfort and love, such as *"I love you, mom. I'm OK."*

At first, Mary Ellen was left feeling very wobbly after a visit from Gene's spirit. In her daily life, Gene was gone. She experienced a huge hole in her life, filled with grief and shock. Yet when Gene came to visit, she would trust more and more that this was somehow an experience of life beyond death. She had one foot in consensus reality, and one "on the other side." Was she crazy?

Mary Ellen found a group of other parents [The Big Circle] who had lost children tragically, and decided to join. To her surprise, they were talking openly about visitations from their children. They were sharing memories about family experiences before the child's death, and listening to their deceased children tell of a dimension beyond description—"3D" and "technicolor" were words they used. They said they existed in a much larger universe filled with Light and Love and the knowledge that they were still very much connected to people they loved on earth.

On the one-year anniversary of Gene's death, Mary Ellen decided to try initiating contact with her son. Up until now, she had always waited for Gene to contact her. She wrote out what she wanted to say, and then she read it to him when he next visited her.

꧁꧂

Hello Gene. I love you and still miss you very much. Having conversations with you has made it easier. Thank you! I want to invite you to Damon's birthday party next week. He'll be 13. He misses you too. I haven't told either of the boys about our conversations. I didn't want to scare them, or have them think I was crazy. But when you visit me, I feel your presence as well as "hear" your thoughts. Please come to the party. Damon will sense your presence on some level, I'm sure. He'll know you're watching out for him. It would be a lovely birthday present.

◦◦◦

The visits from Gene were frequent, and Mary Ellen grew comfortable with the experience and looked forward to them. She told close friends about it, about how the exchanges with Gene left her with feelings of peace and joy. She wondered if maybe they thought she was compensating with fantasies to deal with her loss. But maybe contacting, or being contacted, by spirits once incarnate but now "on the other side" is something the rest of us could do if we tried.

There are tens of thousands of stories recorded in after-death communication research projects, and in personal memoirs that became books. They offer other ways to hold the sudden loss of a beloved child.

Through the ages, indigenous cultures have believed in and experienced conversations with the dead, including ancestors and children. What's necessary is an expansion of consciousness, and a willingness to suspend disbelief, to allow the possibility. Then it often happens.

At Damon's birthday party, Mary Ellen "saw" Gene. No one else did. Damon said spontaneously, "I think Gene's here with us tonight. I can feel him. I love you, bro." And then he blew out the candles.

Commentary

Frances: Mary Ellen, the mother, is a symbol for all of us who lose loved ones. We grieve, we cry, we ask "Why?" when it's sudden, unexpected—especially when it's a child of ours whom we love dearly. A hole is torn in the psyche. The mother feels that she will never be whole again—always a piece missing. The child is there like a phantom limb, but it is not as "real" as a real arm or leg. We feel it, but it isn't the same.

We incarnate and we learn that great lesson: how deeply can we love? The depth of grief tells us how much we can love, how much we can share ourselves with others, become parts of others.

We are all One. We are each divine, and each a particle of God. The extent to which we can heal the hole left by the loss of a beloved, still carry on, still produce a life that is meaningful to ourselves and others—that is the test, that is the lesson of loss. That is one gift of such a loss.

Cynthia: This is very difficult to know, in the days and weeks and months after the loss. Within the past month, ten families in Boulder, Colorado suddenly lost a loved one who had the misfortune to be in a grocery store when a very disturbed individual came in and shot ten people to death.

F: Such enormous pain, such a huge hole will start to heal—or not—for each person affected. A wound cannot help but heal. It is in the nature of the co-creation of life on earth that the healing process commences. It may not heal before the grief-stricken person dies, themselves. It can be slowed down by living in grief and not in love. The Light of Healing is always available—but the individual must want it, must ask for it, act in connection with healing energies.

This story shows the power of connection between your side and our side (what you call "the other side"). There *are* no sides. There is no "inside" and "outside." All of our co-creations flow together, individual yet connected. I am here with you tonight, very present as we create Book Three [of the Greater Reality Series]. I am present—nearby, you might call it—because we are in constant connection. Think of me, call my name, and I am present.

That's why Gene appeared. Mary Ellen called him, asking, "Where are you?" And he appeared. But only because she had the strong feeling he was not dead—that is, disappeared, gone from All That Is. She had the spiritual development necessary to believe Gene was still part of the Whole. And indeed he was, and he appeared. They had a special bond. Not all "deceased" *wish* to connect or reunite with their loved ones from their incarnation. It is painful for them, too. And it can still contain unresolved issues.

C: I know this to be factual. My mother and I had "issues." She passed in 1999, and we've begun meeting "across the veil." We're doing well in making this happen. I already feel much healing, and will continue to make connections to her, honor her for her many contributions to my life, and forgive her trespasses. I ask her often to forgive me for not seeing her pain, her challenges. She and I are exploring these together, now. She is willing to do that, and I ask her forgiveness often.

F: Yes, and you are both healing beautifully. Nothing says that the healing cannot continue when you're in separate dimensions. She is nearby, and she loves you very much. She is overjoyed that the two of you are finding your way to a new level of Wholeness, of being co-created in Love.

So many of the bruises of an earth relationship can be worked on for the benefit of an incarnate and a discarnate from the soul group. The whole soul group rejoices in the healing process.

C: What else can we say about the specific experience of losing a child to disease, or accident, or even suicide? So many teenagers are committing suicide.

F: The loss through suicide is an especially harsh wound to address, even in a lifetime. It is the same healing process but moves much more slowly, because there are usually multiple lifetimes of issues to address and clear away. But the process follows the same pattern you have with your mother. First, create the connection—that is, be open to the dialogue. Then, remember "the good parts" of the relationship as a foundation for the dialogue to follow. Allow the conversation to meander on its own. Stop when recriminations start to come in, from either side. Keep building on the positive memories and create new ones in the present moment. Go to a park together. Spend time with another child in the extended family—one who is troubled, or one who is doing well. That is, create new memories for the two of you. God is Love. Make more of it.

C: Thank you, Frances. What a beautiful idea—create new memories with a beloved who is "on the other side."

I'm having a small ninety-ninth birthday party for my father this week. His spirit left his body eleven years ago. He and I will have a new memory to share.

F: That's a lovely idea.

≈©

As a psychic medium, I have read for hundreds of people...and have connected them to their loved ones who are no longer on this earth. These loved ones offer us a miraculous view of existence and the universe.

— LAURA LYNNE JACKSON, author,
The Light Between Us: Lessons for the Living

Homeless People Welcome

The Light of Purpose

⁓ℯ

Scene: *A homeless person in South Central Los Angeles wants a COVID vaccine shot. Living in a makeshift tent in a hidden corner of a beach is better than dying. It's March 2021, around 45 degrees at night, and lots of rain off and on. Roy wants to live, and he believes his only chance is to find a way to get one of those shots.*

A street social worker explains to Roy that there's a priority list for who gets vaccinated. First on the list are people over 75, then over 65, then healthcare workers, then essential people. Roy doesn't fit any of those categories. He's only 62, been living on the streets for over ten years, thinks he'll make it back to his janitor job any day now. He was good at it. He has no family. His wife took the kids back to her hometown in Georgia when they couldn't make it on her housework jobs alone. And what does "essential" mean?

All Roy knows is that he wants one of those shots. He's not aware that you need two, four weeks apart. He's also doesn't know what an online portal is. He doesn't have a computer or a cell phone, or a car to go to the drive-through vaccination site at Dodger Stadium. He doesn't even have an address.

None of that will soon matter. Roy is about to cross paths with Dr. Jerry Abraham. This is their story.

ials of the COVID vaccine are rolling out of manufacturing centers in the Midwest. Large numbers are headed to California to be distributed throughout the state. Long lines of eligible seniors are standing with their walkers and canes at clinics, drug stores, and various community centers and college campuses that have been pressed into service as vaccine distributors. One of those sites is the Kedren Community Health Center in Lynnwood, a town of about 72,000 people, mostly Black and Brown. Lynnwood has been hard hit by the virus—one in every six residents has caught COVID.

Dr. Jerry Abraham is a family doctor and the director of Kedren Health. He knows that other centers in the state have received initial vaccine supplies. Kedren has not. He calls up the county public health department to find out when his allocation is coming. Kedren wasn't on the list. That is fixed right away and supplies arrive. Jerry, as he's known to the staff, makes sure the vaccines are given out equitably, that vaccines in the predominantly Black and Brown community are going predominantly to Black and Brown people. He carefully ignores the eligibility guidelines.

Roy, who's African American, hears through the homeless grapevine that shots are being given out at Kedren. He panhandles enough change to take a bus, and arrives midafternoon. He knows where the center is because he's been there before for infections and asthma.

As he approaches the center, he sees lines of older folks and hears upbeat music in the background. He sees the new sign on the building:

COVID vaccine shots here.

HOMELESS PEOPLE WELCOME.

Immigration status does not matter.

As Roy stands in line waiting his turn, a volunteer helps him fill in a registration form that's later entered into the county's database. What about Roy's not having a driver's license, or any other kind of ID? The only thing that's relevant is that Roy is a homeless man who wants a COVID vaccine shot. That's all that matters to him. The volunteer enters the information Roy gives her.

After standing in line for several hours, Roy reaches the blue-and-white tents in the parking lot where the shots are being given. He's directed to a vaccination tent, much nicer than his own tent. He's greeted by Jerry.

"Hey bro. How ya doin'?"

"It's not my best day but I'm glad to be here and getting this shot. Gonna save my life."

"This is your lucky day. This will go a long way toward preventing you from getting the virus."

"I seen how people die from it. In the homeless area where I live, I seen people holding their chests, can't breathe, crying for Mama, just like that guy who died from the cop kneeling on his neck, 'I can't breathe!' The EMS truck usually don't make it in time. The guy is dead before they get there. They head to the morgue instead of the hospital."

Dr. Abraham administers the shot. Roy feels a slight sting. It makes him happy. The fear of getting sick lifts. He's given a card that states he's received his first shot. The second one is scheduled for four weeks ahead. He didn't know that this required two shots. He'll have to figure out how to get here again, on the right day. He hopes he doesn't forget.

Later, the doctor is talking with a reporter from the *LA Times*. "They deserve a vaccine just as much as everybody else," Jerry says. "If they come here, they will leave with the vaccine in the arm. It creates a lot of headaches for us to report that information to the county and to the federal government, but we will find a way. It's about access. People don't know where to go and they don't have laptops and cell phones to make appointments." Jerry and a group of other Black doctors and healthcare workers are working to find funding for a fleet of mobile vans in order to take the vaccine door-to-door and to homeless encampments. Maybe the one where Roy lives.

Commentary

Frances: I happen to know that Dr. Abraham — Jerry — experienced the terrors of the streets. As a Black teenager in south LA, he knows how frightened one can get if you don't have a home, a definite next meal, and when existence is a day-to-day struggle with others who also want to survive. You can't focus on the future when the present is all you have. Roy had a job, a family and his dignity. All that evaporated when the school where he worked had its budget cut. One of the two janitors had to go. The Roy in our story was told to leave.

His life was not grand, but he had a job that had positive aspects. The students liked and respected him. He was part of a community. He was "essential" in a way not included in the COVID vaccine priority lists. Technically, it means people who keep basic services running. Isn't keeping a school clean and its systems maintained "essential"? With COVID, the school shut down and Roy would have been laid off anyway. But when he was laid off, the school was still functioning.

"Not essential" is a terrible way to categorize a human being. We are each essential in the divine scheme of things. Each one is essential in the evolution of the co-creative dance of space/time reality. We are each a particle of the expanse of Love and Light, moving in harmony and counterpoint.

Dr. Abraham is one of those chosen few who made it out of a downtrodden early history and into college and medical school. He had to work very hard to get through school. What is not seen is the purpose he chose for this lifetime—struggle against great odds to become a role model for others. All by himself? Hardly. Jerry had plenty of help from ancestors, spirit guides, adults who saw the potential the teenager had to "make it" with much outside help—incarnate and spiritual.

It was Jerry's commitment to purpose—become a doctor, minister to his people. And when COVID came along, it was clear to him that his purpose was to get vaccines to those without resources. Jerry did not see them as "non-essential" people.

Cynthia: And we could say that Roy's purpose to stay alive co-created the Hedrin clinic scenario where Jerry could fulfill his purpose. Roy also reminds us how resilient we humans are. To go from a normal lifestyle to living in a tent on a beach in LA for over ten years! I hope we can co-create a more compassionate world where an individual's health and safety are paramount.

F: It's all co-creation—so many individual souls in motion to create and collaborate in the dance of existence on earth. All the while watched over by the myriad soul groups—whose members are carrying on the learning for each soul group. All members benefit—incarnate or not. That adds energy to Roy's and Jerry's abilities to maintain their commitments to each other and the Whole—to all of us.

At the end of our story, Jerry was looking to add others to his shining purpose. Looking for a mobile van outfitted to deliver vaccines in neighborhoods and where homeless people are sheltered. That allows more people to participate. It's a purpose that excites the hearts of onlookers. Many want to contribute to this higher purpose, and do. The mobile van becomes a reality—a co-creation that manifests the Love that is available to help fuel all kinds of noble enterprises, and does.

C: I read a more recent story about LA COVID vaccines. It says that the large-scale vaccine centers were shutting down and they've shifted to mobile clinics. Undoubtedly, Dr. Abraham was instrumental in making that happen.

F: That underscores our point: Don't give up on your dreams. Understand that when something beautiful comes together—a large public work of art, a response to a social cause, a new wing of a hospital—the deep underlying energy of creation is called forth, is summoned, as it were, by the deep, spiritual purpose of the participants. Its manifestation may be visible, but its underpinning, its foundation, is sourced in the power of All That Is. A visionary gets credit, and deserves to be recognized for his or her role—but never lose sight of the fact that all manifestations of the dance of Light and Love come from the Source—all of us in concert.

The point is to let go of the attachment to a space/time reality—very difficult to do without effort. But now there are many people—writers, poets and musicians, to name a few—who have offered a roadmap through the phenomenal world (world of interacting objects and cause-and-effect events) and see it for what it is—a movie, as we described in Book Two. A compelling movie, a movie that can move heart and soul with joy or tragedy beyond bearable. But [what's needed is] learning to straddle both worlds—the earthbound unfolding story of your life as you're living it, and the consciousness that you are watching it unfold in ways that serve your purpose and ways that don't.

What you want, ideally, is for your consciousness to inform your life and for your life to expand your consciousness beyond what you came into your incarnation with. The interplay dynamic, when in good balance, is a happy and fulfilling life. But it's easy to get derailed—either by your own self-created distractions, or by the huge distractions going on right now on earth—the pandemic, and the cry for social justice in America. The outpouring of so many people marching in the streets with the risk of virus hanging over them is marvelous and heartening.

C: You mentioned "soul talent" in an earlier session. What is "soul talent?"

F: It's a way of growing one's Self, of deepening a core value. The hero's action, or a piece of music, or a performance by a dancer is the exterior experience, the demonstration that something is being perfected. But it's the *interior* experience, the creativity—co-creativity, in most cases—that solidifies the soul's understanding of the depth of God's creations. We are all furthering the expansion of Love and Light into an infinite number of dimensions. Each "talent," if you will, is simply the gateway, the soul's choice of venue for the learning of co-creation to take place. Is that clear?

C: Yes, and beautiful. What about all those souls who have left their incarnations because of the virus, or maybe now because of the dangerous situations on the streets of major cities? You've convinced me they are martyrs and heroes, yet not recognized as such.

F: Recognition is an ephemeral thing. Nice for people who are still alive or grieving a lost loved one, but not so necessary for the soul who is now free to watch the show from the balcony. Gratitude is one of the Lights along the way to a deeper understanding of the purpose of an earthly incarnation.

The brave souls who are dying from COVID are leading the way. They are messengers, in a sense, by their willingness to go forward in the vanguard of people whose dying will be remembered as exemplary, as heroic in the sense of willing to die first in the pandemic. It's never easy, never blissful.

C: What can we say to those who are holding out hope and say we must not give in to despair? Who say a new age is possible?

F: It *is* possible. A new and more balanced period will come. What you and our readers and those who know what's coming are doing is ALL TO THE GOOD. Nothing is lost.

But it is not for you to sort out which scenario will prevail. None of you will be incarnate as you are now. Those of us who are your future are only trying to spare you some pain, some grief. Visionaries see "a promised land." The promised land is not within the grasp of current inhabitants of Earth. It is across the bridge, "on the other side."

The sea rises, the light fails, lovers cling to each other, and children cling to us. The moment we cease to hold each other, the moment we break faith with one another, the sea engulfs us and the light goes out.

—JAMES BALDWIN (1924-1987),
author and poet, "For Nothing Is Fixed"

— *Story 6* —

Starving Children Don't Cry

The Light of Being

⟞⟎

Scene: *It's spring, 2021. The Za'atari refugee camp is located in Jordan on its border with Syria. It has been taking in people fleeing the Syrian civil war since the war started in 2011. The camp has grown from a collection of tents to a semi-permanent city holding around 80,000 Syrians, half of them children. Dozens of international agencies have collaborated to create a living environment, with greenhouses growing organic vegetables, wastewater treatment plants, and water lines connecting the small housing structures to fresh water. Most Syrians who end up at Za'atari want to go home, but their villages no longer exist. They've been demolished in the ongoing war involving the Syrian government, ISIS, the pro-democracy forces, the United States, and Russia.*

It is in this refugee camp that we meet Ingrid and Hassan. Their story is a microcosm of the pain, compassion, hostility and collaboration that are the crosscurrents of 21st-century life on earth.

ngrid is a young Norwegian woman who has been trained by the Norwegian Refugee Council to be a staff person at Za'atari. However, no amount of training could have prepared someone for what just happened. A young Syrian mother who'd been traveling for days with her six-month-old son, Hassan, has been directed to the camp's clinic. She hands Hassan to Ingrid, whispers his name, and says, "Please" in Arabic. Ingrid replies, "I will take care of him." The mother collapses on the floor and dies within a few hours from dehydration.

Hassan is listless and weighs less than half of what he should weigh at his age. He doesn't have enough energy to cry for food. His body is cannibalizing his organs and they are badly damaged. He's given emergency treatment, but it's too late. He dies in Ingrid's arms. She has kept her promise to the mother—she took care of Hassan until he left his body.

Each day, Ingrid is witness to the chaos and suffering that intertwine war, famine, disease, and hopelessness. She also sees the immense waves of compassion and commitment that rise to the occasion. That's what keeps her going day after day, Hassan after Hassan. She has learned that you cannot save every child. It's not for her to know why one lives and one dies. Her spiritual beliefs tell her that she and Hassan are One. Different aspects of the All That Is. His pain is her pain. His joy at being held and loved, if only briefly, was her joy too.

Now, Ingrid hands off Hassan's body to someone trained to give a Muslim boy a proper burial ritual. She must move on to teaching her class at Oasis, a program for young women refugees. There they learn skills that can lead to employment outside the camp, such as tailoring and hairdressing. Graduates receive equipment needed to sustain their skills and start their own businesses. Oasis is very popular among the girls because it offers a space for them to learn about leadership and sense of self. They also enjoy time together in games and sports. Their joy becomes Ingrid's joy. It's what keeps her going when the inevitable deaths occur.

Today, she's also being tested by a brother of one of the Oasis participants. He doesn't want his sister to learn a skill or to think she can become independent in any way. It's contrary to his beliefs about the roles women should play. Ingrid carefully handles the angry young man by saying that she will set up a counseling session for him and his sister with a skilled mediator who understands both sides of that story. The sister agrees.

That evening, Ingrid goes to her room and sets up a ritual that helps her get through the loss of Hassan and his mother. She imagines both the mother and Hassan crossing the bridge to the other side. The mother arrives first and is welcomed by a crowd of relatives and ancestors with open hearts. She is honored by those shouting, "Praise be to Allah" for her heroic journey to bring Hassan to Za'atari. All her trials of her former incarnation are over. She anxiously asks how Hassan is doing. Her grandmother says, "He will be here soon." She is both crushed at the news that Hassan won't stay alive, and overjoyed that he will join her.

Then Hassan shows up, now free of malnutrition and with a head full of curly black hair. "Mama, mama!" Hassan says, and she realizes he's much happier here than he would have been in the refugee clinic, even with the best of care.

Ingrid has learned from her stay at Za'atari that life is impermanent, and that tragedy has as much to teach her as joy and beauty. She believes that life teaches us about impermanence and that we each die many times. That when we die, we enter into a greater reality where pain and tragedy are over and where we get to see the larger purpose for that lifetime. Ingrid has learned how to be present in each moment, in each encounter of the day. Seeing deaths every day has lessened her fear of death.

She often hears from family and friends how "selfless" she is to be volunteering in a refugee camp. Maybe there is some of that. But she knows how very fortunate she is to be volunteering in a camp where she gets to grow in consciousness each day and to strengthen her connection to the Whole and to her life's purpose.

Hassan and his mother see Ingrid doing her ritual, and they send much love and gratitude to her. She receives the blessings. Her tears are not for Hassan or his mother. They water the garden of her soul, where Love and Tranquility flourish—just what Ingrid needs to continue her work in the camp the next day.

Commentary

Cynthia: What do you have to say about Ingrid and Hassan?

Frances: They are connected in a dance of co-creation. Together, they teach us about suffering and compassion. The linkage between the two, and the necessity of one for the other.

Compassion is a beautiful soul characteristic. It must be cultivated in the right soil, in the right environment where there can be a balance of suffering and the opportunities to be of service. Hassan loves his mother, and in the brief time he has left between losing his mother and leaving his body as well, he has the experience of Ingrid. What a strange and wonderful event. A Syrian baby, never going to reach childhood, is held in a loving embrace by a woman from Norway. What does the image conjure up? Mother and Child. [It's] a connection that is seen as primary, symbolic of all the deepest connections two souls can hold together.

As we demonstrated in Story 4, "Love Calls," the connection [between mother and child] stays intact even if the child dies first. Here we have the Syrian mother, traveling from her village to a Jordanian refugee camp, her energy almost entirely derived from her love for Hassan. How does she feel handing him to a white woman with blond hair? Does it at all matter? No, not at all. The mother senses the deep mothering-soul of Ingrid and knows that it transcends any cultural differences.

Those are the kinds of exchanges that can heal the fractured connections that have come to dominate relationships between humans on earth. Color, race, gender, nationality, sexual orientation—all have come to bar the deep communion we really have with one another. The differences are so superficial, so unnecessary.

C: How do you account for these identifiers getting in the way of true human-to-human bonding?

F: One answer has to do with the fear that is rampant on the planet right now. Fear that is rooted in real concern for survival of the species itself. "Who will be there with me when the chaos, when the various crises from climate change and economic collapse hit?" It's already happening, as you know. Bonds of race and age peers and locality will mean a lot more than they do now during those upheavals.

But it will be so much better for those who see their basic humanity as the most foundational for getting through those upheavals. There are possibilities for sharing each other's pain, and offering support to those impacted by violence and hatred that have been unleashed in the face of growing disintegration.

C: Domestic violence has increased, also. Child abuse, and I'm sure even animal abuse, has increased—all due to the frustrations set loose by fear.

F: Humans are not that far along in their evolution. They revert to aggression and violence to quell their fears. Physical strength is a bulwark against fear. Compassion—heart-to-heart connection—is so much better a response. Humans are in transition, and our [Greater Reality] books are a small part of the many candles lighting the way.

C: Anything else we can say about Story 6?

F: What comes out of this period of imbalance and impermanence, movement toward a way of being in harmony as a species, remains to be seen. Various probable realities are jockeying to be the emergent one for most current inhabitants. So much depends on the Wisdom Teachers who emerge from a shared vision of what is the desired scenario for humanity's next phase.

The technological thrusts run counter to the qualities of compassion and joy and connection. They [social media] may facilitate connections in some ways, but they do not foster it. Again, human-to-human relationships, Ingrid-to-Hassan, point the way. Its setting in a refugee camp is a dramatic way to underscore what it takes to break the addiction to the materialism, social media, and mindless entertainment that dominates now.

C: I'm reminded of an image that was seared into my mind when a friend told me a story of a family she knew that didn't have enough money to feed the children adequately. The mother was trying to do her best, but one night all she had was a box of Cheerios and no milk. Each child got a bowl of Cheerios and water. She sat them down in front of the TV to give herself a break. A commercial for a big juicy hamburger came on, loaded with cheese and tomatoes and the usual trimmings. The five-year-old said, "Mommy, Mommy, I want one of those. Can I have one of those?"

Now when I see a commercial for a burger, or a pizza, or an enchilada, I think about all the children who are eating Cheerios and water and would love to have one of those. According to my Congresswoman, Barbara Lee, there are at least 100,000 children in her district in the East Bay of San Francisco who don't get enough to eat. It puts an entirely different spin on those fast-food commercials for me.

F: Yes, indeed. And that clarity can help to light the way to a greater Light of Being surrounding everyone.

C: The Light of Being—I like that. Say more.

F: Imagine a giant light bulb capable of shining brighter and brighter when fed by the compassion and love of those who truly understand, or are moving toward that understanding, as you are, adding their energy to its power to reach all the beings on the planet. It is a planetary project. Let the Light in [in] the forms of food and shelter and teachings of all kinds—sports, literature, crafts, etc. A world filled with beings who want to share their unique talents and learn from others. In order to do that, basic needs of all beings need to be met. And all in harmony with the surrounding environment. A huge undertaking, but it can be done. There are small-scale examples going on everywhere. Make it the norm, not the exception. Make Love the currency of the realm, not wealth or fame.

Start with a creed, a credo that is taught to children all over the world. It wouldn't be that difficult to convince everyone of a basic credo of how to live your life while incarnate. And then each person would want to do as much as she or he could to fulfill that commitment while here. All the while knowing that, at some point, your soul will move on.

Boundless Compassion reaches out to those who are suffering, to those who are being persecuted for race or ethnicity, or for being poor and vulnerable. There is more than enough Compassion to cover and alleviate all suffering on planet Earth. But not the will to do it yet. But as we can see, it's growing every day in so many different places.

Just as we welcome a new baby into the world and say goodbye to a soul that has left, we must honor each individual. If we make each one sacred, special, to be nurtured and supported in reaching his/her potential, we won't make as many of them [babies]. Quality rather than quantity, to use an old phrase.

I plan to return soon to an incarnation. I will be one of those babies who arrives with promise and energy and creative talents. My community will regard me, and all the other babies that arrive, as special beings, here for the purpose of nurturing and co-creating a new world of love and beauty. So each baby must be treated as sacred. You can't do that if you have too many to care for.

Not each human needs to co-create a new person. [There is] plenty of work to go around in growing and supporting the ones who show up. "It takes a village to raise a child" will again become common sense. The goodness that resides in some people's hearts—the compassion, empathy, wanting to serve—that's an aspect of the greater reality, too. It's a glimpse of "the beloved community," the oversoul group, the home of the eternal that people can have while incarnate.

The pandemic [current COVID] is a Teacher—a harsh one, to be sure. But her lessons will be regarded as messages of change, of direction, of rebalance. Look for them. They are springing up all over. Your world, and soon mine again, will not be based on fossil fuels, or new technologies or AI, or anything else that is not from the hearts and souls of its inhabitants. If innovators show up—and they will—they must fit into the scheme of things, which is the Love and the Light of realization that we are all One.

C: Will there be a future in which to remember? I'm thinking of climate change, and economic collapse on the horizon as well.

F: We'll have to see how much of the current material reality remains intact after the dissipative period is over. I don't know. There are so many probably realities on the horizon. It will be decided by what kinds of leaders, visionaries, and healers show up during the chaotic period. It's open-ended.

~⚬~

The day will come when, after harnessing space, the winds, the tides and gravitation, we shall harness for God the energies of Love. And on that day, for the second time in the history of the world, we shall have discovered Fire.

—PIERRE TEILHARD DE CHARDIN (1881-1955),
French Jesuit priest, scientist, and philosopher

Time to Go Home

The Light Showing the Way Home

≫℘

Scene: *A hospice hospital room in a small town in the Midwest. Dana is already drifting just outside her body but has not entirely disengaged from her physical self. She is having a difficult time letting the body "be" without her Spirit.*

Her lifelong friend Regina, a medium and transition counselor, is with her. Regina had brought with her the manuscript for Seven Questions About Life After Life that Cynthia Spring had asked her to review before the book's publication. This is how Regina came to know Frances Vaughan, the co-creator of the book.

Frances offered to be with Dana and Regina in the room, and Regina welcomed her presence. Regina tells us the story.

I was with Dana as she began her morphine late Wednesday evening. Thursday, she was still very present and in a great deal of pain. Her hands, feet, and forearms swelled from the blood pooling. The leukemia was raging inside as fever and infection took hold.

The hospice nurse would not increase the morphine, believing Dana would want to be more awake for today's Thanksgiving and be with her family and friends and possibly enjoy some pumpkin pie. I honestly don't know what the nurse was thinking. Food was not what Dana wanted, and I was her only family present. The pain and morphine made her nauseous to the point of vomiting.

As I sat with Dana, as she was drifting in and out, I wondered about her family—all the relatives who had previously passed. I slightly sensed a few of them present nearby, as though they were behind a foggy window watching her. Yet I could also feel Frances ever so present with me in the room. She guided me through Dana's journey, and I was grateful.

Frances told me that Dana was fighting to stay with her body. Dana was afraid. She believed that she might not deserve Heaven. Here we were, Thanksgiving. It was hard for Dana, as she thought that maybe, just maybe, she would not be received into Jesus' arms.

Dana asked me to play one of her healing CDs. I flipped through the several she had next to her bed. Their titles were not of blessing and love but of repentance and fear of sin: fire and brimstone. But I obliged.

Frances kept telling me to give Dana whatever she requested; this time would be short. She told me *they* were preparing her family on the other side for Dana's arrival. Frances told me many of my friend's deceased family members were in the astral-field energy bandwidth—close to the

Earth. Her father and brother, who had passed years earlier, were waiting to take their beloved Dana home; but she searched for others, especially her mother.

I stayed with Dana the length of the day. The pain was evident on her face as she groaned with each movement of her body. I kept reading the *Seven Questions* manuscript, sometimes aloud or quietly to myself. It was unbearable to leave Dana this Thanksgiving night. I asked Frances if Dana would die tonight. She comforted me that Dana would still be here in the morning. Her mind wasn't ready to leave yet.

If there is a Purgatory, I was positive Dana existed in it, right there in the room. The swelling had increased throughout her body. Her mouth and nose had begun bleeding. She opened her eyes only to acknowledge that I was present. She cried for more pain relief. Fortunately, the hospice nurse, per the doctor's prescription, increased her morphine substantially—relief for dear Dana was finally on its way.

The morphine took effect almost immediately. As Dana settled into her deep sleep, I tried to rest my mind. I was letting go of the one friend in my life who had been with me since I was five years old. Warm tears filled my eyes.

When I left Dana that evening, I wasn't sure if she would be with us in the morning. I debated sleeping in the recliner next to her. I had promised Dana I wouldn't leave her until she had left her body, and here I was, leaving her. But Frances assured me once again, "Go and get a good night's rest. Tomorrow you will be needed."

Dana was sleeping when I arrived the next morning. Drifting in and out of consciousness. I could sense that her body and Spirit were beginning to separate. Her Spirit was more prominent than her body. The Spirit was opaque, not crystal clear and bright, as Frances appears. I was hoping that

Dana might be a bit further along. My own sense of what I thought should be a straightforward process was more like a fight or a last stand for Dana. I suddenly felt rather selfish.

Arguments were drifting over her as she lay there. I could hear Dana pleading with her higher self. Testifying to her humble life while still maintaining she did everything expected of her. How could she leave with a clear mind and heart if she still felt she was undeserving? Dana had lived a life of servitude: for her parents, her siblings, her church, and her God. Service was how she managed every day. But now, she was questioning her service, convinced that her leukemia was punishment for her sins. Somehow, she thought, she had failed God and was now unworthy to enter into His Home.

Dana was determined to live, even as her body was collapsing and her organs began to fail. Septicemia was in full swing. She was fighting hard to stay with her body all the way to the end.

"Bring in hospice clergy," Frances said to me.

Within an hour, the cleric had arrived. I was grateful, as Dana's Spirit was fully engaged in her body. When the minister entered through the door, I could see the Bible in his hand. I was hoping this was not more of the "Repent and be saved" that I'd been hearing on Dana's healing CD. Frances assured me that this man was a man of Divine love. I could feel it as soon as he shook my hand. Dana hadn't much time left on this earthly plane, and we needed to get her physically ready to release her Spirit.

"Gregory" was how he introduced himself. "Hospice clergy. No religion is attached."

Frances stepped in and began channeling through me. I knew this wasn't me speaking, as words were coming fast yet gentle as I covered our intros regarding Dana and her physical journey. She was only 67. Too young. Her mom had only recently passed, two years prior.

Gregory wanted to know my past, and I obliged, allowing the words "healing hands," "death and dying," and "near-death" to pass over my lips. Frances wanted me to be honest about who I am. She encouraged me to say more. I spoke of Dana's father being present in the room, as I could smell his Camel cigarettes, and her eldest brother was with us too.

"How do *I* see them?" Gregory inquired. And so the door opened for me to come forward and share more about Spirit, about the God Love within us: the Self God Love, and the Everywhere God Love. How can they be separate? I told Gregory about a manuscript I was reading, scripted through automatic writing by Cynthia Spring in session with Frances Vaughan.

Then Frances stepped in and, through me, excitedly shared about the afterlife that awaited Dana. I could sense the excitement in Gregory and his curiosity. Here he had been called to counsel Dana and me, but Frances and I were teaching him instead. He was bursting with questions for Frances, and she obliged with deliberate and straightforward answers. There was no wavering or uncertainty. The strength of her absolute divine love penetrated every corner of the room and spoke to Gregory's inner core belief. He overflowed with gratitude.

Hungry for more, Gregory then asked me to show him how I work when a deceased family member is in the room and ready to receive their loved one to the other side. I got up and moved to Dana's side. Brushing her moist skin fevered in disease, I spoke gently to Dana.

"Dana, your brother Lantz is here. He is here to take you out of your body. He does not want you to fear anything.

He says you do not recognize him, as he no longer has cerebral palsy. He is a little over six feet, about the same size as when he died, but his body stands straight and tall. He looks about 24, when he would have been at his prime. And he has a swimmer's physique. He always liked the water. Especially the beach.

"Lantz knows how much you've wanted to get back to the beach and wants you to know that he will take you to California so that you both can get into the Pacific Ocean. You can feel the hot sand on your feet and sense the warm sun on your skin. He knows how much you like this."

"Lantz is here to take you over," I continued. "You can trust him, Dana. He is here to bring you love. He wants you to really know love. That's all that matter right now. He is here to take you home." Even in Dana's morphine-induced sleep, I knew she could hear me. She was listening and so much wanted to believe me. But still, she had doubt.

"I can't go yet," I heard her say. She begged me, "Please, I need forgiveness. I am so sorry for all I have sinned against God."

I asked Gregory to move forward. "Please," I said to him, "she's asking for forgiveness."

Gregory opened his Bible and began to read from it. He spoke of God's forgiveness and His unconditional love. "Our Father...," he prayed, "... For thine is the kingdom and the power and the glory. Amen."

Dana finally began to release. I could feel her slip out a bit more from her body.

I asked Gregory to place his right hand over Dana's heart and take my right hand with his left. Lifting my left hand open palm upward, I told him I would ask to receive a power of love and light through my left hand. This power would travel into my right hand and then into his left hand and over to the hand he laid on Dana. I told him he was now going to feel the power of unconditional love. Gregory bowed his head in earnest to receive. At that moment, I could feel Frances put her hand into my left palm. The immensity of her love from its source was sensational. Gregory looked at me and asked, "Do you feel that?" His eyes were wide with wonder.

"Yes," I answered. "This is the flow of infinite love. Just allow it to move into Dana. She is ready to receive." With that, we continued to send the energy, the immensity, the love that Frances poured into us for the next few minutes. Gregory welcomed this, as did Dana. Her body drank in this outpouring of love. Dana's life spirit was grateful for this precious time, as was I. And then I could feel Frances remove her hand from mine. I released Gregory's hand. He sat back in his chair, stunned by what he just experienced.

"I feel 'charged,' energized," he commented. "I always knew there was more, but I could never put my finger on it."

Looking at Dana, we reflected on her face; the grimace of pain no longer blanketed her.

I heard Dana say, "Thank you." With that, Gregory said he did not want to leave her side. He wanted to bask in what had just happened. Frances gently nudged me to let him know that he could carry this with him always.

"This isn't a one-time fleeting moment of Divine Love, but an endless river that will flow as long as you wish," Frances counseled, "as long as the flow is allowed to do just that, to flow. It is not something you hold on to and keep for yourself only, as it can only be in its wholeness as an endless river. Acknowledging this is the 'beginning' to the flow."

With his newfound energy, Gregory might as well have been floating out the room. His step was light and free.

"Frances," I said to her, "we did good work together. And I thank you."

"Now," she replied, "let's read to Dana the final two chapters of my book. Out loud," she insisted.

And so I did. Out loud. Dana's Spirit stood at her body's side. She wasn't ready to leave quite yet. She was now wanting to hear a little more. And so I began....

> *"Question 6. How does one live with the knowledge*
> *that there is life after life?"*

I read until the closing chapter's final page, "*Question 7. Where is home?*" was complete, and those last words were heard by Dana.

> **"Death is a transition to another form of**
> **existence. ...**
>
> **Let your star shine!"**

I closed the pages of the manuscript and slid it back into its now-torn and worn brown envelope.

"Well, Dana," I said to no one but her energy, "it's time for you to take Lantz's hand. There are so many more things for you to know, and you can't learn them here in this room. I will watch over your body, for it is only the vessel from which you lived this life on Earth. It is broken, like a fragile cracked vase that no longer holds water. It's time to go home."

I felt her step back and move into love as her Spirit passed through the outdoor wall to meet her brother. Her father joined them. I was left in the empty and darkened room, curtains drawn closed as they had been for two days now.

I opened them up. I looked down at Dana's body; her face was soft and her breathing steady. Dana was no longer there.

I stayed with her body for a long while. I was thankful for Frances' assistance. It was her "first" assist to the other side. I could tell she felt grateful to me as well, for my trust in her. "There is so much to learn about all this," she said.

"Yes, Frances," I said aloud. "Yes, indeed." Three hours later, Dana's body took its final breath.

Commentary

Cynthia: What would you like to say about this story?

Frances: I am so grateful, blessed to have been part of Dana's passing. It was such an honor, my first experience of being present in that way. Regina's skills and my higher vantage point combined to offer Dana the best possible combination of an unconditional love from Regina and the promise of rejoining her soulmates and truly going home in its profound sense.

Dana's mother didn't want to be present in the room. She felt she would slow the process down and she and Dana would "take up time" in an earthly reunion, when their heavenly one would be so much more joyful and pain-free. It was. I was allowed to be present as a witness and welcoming spirit.

C: The process of letting Spirit separate from the body as described by Regina seems like a typical push/pull that many incarnates experience during their dying time.

F: Yes, it's a cliché but it's true that dying is much more difficult than being dead. When people say they fear death, it's often that rending asunder [of] the Spirit and the Body that they fear. And with good reason. It can be more powerful than the body's painful demise.

C: Why is that?

F: When the Body senses it's going to lose its vitality, its "aliveness," it's understandably shaken to its foundation. Its anchor in space/time is going to be severed. All forms of Life want to continue, until they have to let go. "Don't leave me. Please don't leave me," the Body cries. And the Spirit gently says, "I must."

That's not true of every person's death-transition process. There are those few who have prepared themselves for the transition, studied the ancient texts, know what to expect. Others have done it so many times, leaving from so many lifetimes, that they know the territory, so to speak. But those few "enlightened ones" are still a small minority.

Some people leave their bodies way before they are declared dead. The Body carries on in a kind of limbo, still having bodily functions, often no brain function and no Spirit to enliven the body. Just matter, carrying on the functions it knows, a body on automatic pilot.

C: And the Spirit has moved on, gone back home?

F: Yes, exactly.

C: Please say more about Home.

F: Home is where the heart is. Your spirit returns to its soul group to relax from its arduous trip into physical form and space/time reality. As we've said in the earlier books, Earth is a difficult place to negotiate for any soul, even the most evolved of those who choose to incarnate again. Eventually, reincarnation is not necessary and one remains in a higher frequency not suitable for matter.

C: What about surroundings, forms, on the "other side"?

F: As I shared with you in Books One and Two, you co-create whatever reality you'd like. When I first crossed, I wanted a garden and environment similar to what I had on Earth. And that's what I had. But I quickly realized that was only a transitional phase and I didn't need my Earth "simulation" or, in today's jargon, "virtual reality."

C: You and I met for a while in a spectacular garden setting with a white gazebo.

F: Yes, wasn't that marvelous? Both of us love flowers so much. But we both discovered we didn't need that facade either. Meeting as two brightly shining beings was all the form we needed, as we are now. Some souls enjoy the co-creation of various living spaces modeled on the best of Earth's beautiful places. But they too tire of the same old surroundings and move on to a more rarified existence without Earth forms.

C: What else can you say about the early stages of transition?

F: We covered quite a lot in the earlier books. Life Review, and if necessary, rehab facilities where beings who had a damaging lifestyle or violent ending may rest and receive unconditional love. And as I described, there are those who chose not to join the wondrously expansive existence "on the other side" but instead choose to make their own visions of hell. That's beyond the scope of these books.

C: Regina says you have told her you've been involved in assisting in other transitions since your presence at Dana's transition.

F: Yes, I find my psychotherapy skills—my incarnate profession when I was Frances Vaughan—have been very helpful to those transition counselors who are assisting in the death process. I've been working with the minister who asked for help in his work. But he hasn't totally accepted my existence or the existence of a greater reality, as we speak of it. He is a good man and is doing important work in his community. Maybe someday he'll teach a class on afterlife and ask me to join him. [Smile]

C: Anything else you'd like to say about Story 7?

F: This book has been a delight to co-create with you. Each story carries a theme planted in Books One and Two. Each story is well crafted and carries a message important to our readers. I think in Story 7, we come full circle to the opening of Book One where we ask the question: *Am I more than my physical body?* If a reader has taken the time to read Books One and Two, and done some of the exercises suggested, and really tried to be spiritually nourished by the content, that person is well on his or her way to a much easier transition at the end of the Earth incarnation.

Also equally important is the knowledge that we are conscious beings, first and foremost, sharing our existence far beyond material reality. If we've planted those seeds well, and nurtured them with the materials drawn from so many reinforcing sources, they will bear the fruit of the kind of wise and compassionate beings that Earth so desperately needs in her time of radical rebalance. Many millions will be needed.

Many millions have been preparing many lifetimes, as you and I have, to be of assistance amid the upheavals that are sure to come. The power of recognizing our own divinity, our own roles in the co-creation of limitless realities—putting that larger frame on the upheavals will be so comforting.

It also allows the pain and grief to be alleviated. Let's see how much we can be a part of that momentum.

And the stories we've told, as insightful as they are, offer only hints of the aliveness and grandeur of what's awaiting "on the other side."

The river needs to take the risk

of entering the ocean

because only then will fear disappear,

because that's where the river will know it's not about

disappearing into the ocean,

but of becoming the ocean.

—Kahlil Gibran (1883-1933),
poet, author, and artist

Epilogue

Don't Confine Yourself to a Limited Dimension

What has been my motivation in searching for, and entering, a Greater Reality than ordinary life? This is what Frances Vaughan, my co-author and dear friend, asked me to share with our readers. These days, of course, "ordinary life" has more than its share of joys and tragedies.

To begin to answer this question, I had to go back to journals I had kept, books I had read, and experiences I'd had in workshops and elsewhere. Frances has informed me that I've stretched myself further than I originally believed possible. She asked me to discover: Why? What purpose did this have for me?

I've always been interested in seeing "the bigger picture," in understanding the context of why things happen the way they do. And so I was drawn to learn about what lies beyond the "ordinary reality" that we experience each day, and how we interact with forces that we cannot see but sense are there. That curiosity took me to psychic-development classes in the 1980s (although I didn't show any aptitude), and to read books on near-death experiences (NDEs) and out-of-body experiences (OBEs).

I've heard enough and seen enough evidence to believe that extraterrestrials exist—even the US government has corroborated many reports—but that doesn't seem to impact my life directly. In the 1970s, I read the Seth books channeled by Jane Roberts and came to understand that the universe is trying out so many experiments with life forms, and that maybe humans are experiments, too.

In January 2018, my husband and I attended a lecture by San Francisco Bay Area psychologist Matthew McKay, whose beloved son, Jordan, had been murdered in a robbery several years earlier. Dr. McKay spoke about contacting his son through a technique called after-death communication (ADC) and how successful it had been. He gave us simple instructions and suggested that we try it. My friend Frances Vaughan, a transpersonal psychologist, had passed several months earlier, so it felt natural to try out this form of communication with her. She and I connected easily—and here we are, five years later, completing a trilogy of books together.

How has my experience with the greater reality changed me and benefitted me? When I began channeling Frances and learning about her world of unimaginable variety and co-creation, I saw what a limited dimension I inhabited. The greater reality offers us many more opportunities to experience a variety of physical and spirit forms. But why do we *need* to explore those other forms while we have our hands full simply trying to live on Earth? Because our lives on this planet become so much richer when enhanced by the knowledge that we exist beyond space and time.

What a relief to know that we are more than our physical bodies, more than our finite minds. We can replace much of our fear with love when we look through a larger frame. This does not mean that we must override or ignore the challenges and pains that are part of life on Earth. Frances and I do not question, as an example, that the death of loved ones can be an incredibly painful experience—"The excruciating presence of an absence" was how author Aldous Huxley described it. But knowing that you will be in contact with your loved ones again creates an enormous difference in perspective, feeling and trust, rather than believing that you are cut off from each other forever.

Death is a transition. That's one thing you learn when you begin to examine all the research on near-death experiences. Tens of thousands of NDE stories have been collected by researchers, who hear tales of magnificent and loving episodes told by people who are at a crossroads because of accident or disease—whether to die and go forward or to stay alive and return to their bodies. The ones who tell such stories are those who return to their incarnation to carry out some unfinished purpose. The researchers who put the storytellers' accounts together create a (literally) out-of-this-world scenario. I received my introduction to NDEs through Raymond Moody's 1976 book, *Life After Life*. Having a human experience on Earth is one way to get a workout in mortality—that is, every incarnate being on this planet dies. If you don't care to dwell on what you deem too difficult a topic, then wait for another lifetime to come along when you're ready.

When Frances and I began our work on Book Three, I was delighted to hear that this time, the format was *stories*. The "seven questions" format had served us well in Books One and Two by providing content, then raising questions that readers might have. However, for Book Three, Frances made it clear that our format would be storytelling, the oldest form of human education. I was to choose and shape the stories for Book Three.

It took seven months of channeling sessions with Frances just to bring me to the point where I felt that I could actually do this project. Then I began researching stories for possible inclusion. It took a year longer than I had expected to complete the book, and the obstacles weren't all due to book-related challenges. There was also a worldwide pandemic, a small version of a world war, a huge spike in climate-change events, and my own need to attend to a health issue that required back surgery. All this took place in the middle of Book Three. This was a test of my understanding of the Greater Reality material so far. From what you've read and received in this book, how do you think I did?

Frances' questions as to my motivation persisted. In her gentle way, she still wanted to know why I sat down one day and tried to channel her messages to a broader audience. My response is that a message about what happens after our bodies die seems like crucial information to have any time, but especially these days, as we get hit with one upheaval after another. As I write this, many millions of people are watching TV and seeing dead bodies lying in the streets of Ukraine by the hundreds.

What Frances and I are offering here is not a new way to believe that the Greater Reality exists in a huge variety of forms and frequencies. Instead, we are offering a new way of *Being* in that expanded existence. In Book Two, we quoted the oft-quoted saying: "We are spiritual beings having a human experience." Each story in Book Three provides a threshold to a human experience, as well as details on the spiritual insights that come with it.

To embark on an exploration of the Greater Reality while still incarnate in human form says much about where you are on your personal journey through other dimensions of existence. Even the wise and kind teachers by our side, as I am privileged to have with Frances, know just how little they understand.

Perhaps my ultimate response to Frances' initial question about why I have given myself to this journey into the Greater Reality is that, at the time, I don't know if I recognized why I moved toward a particular teacher, an organizational form, or a compelling presentation. There was always simply a "rightness" to it. It was the next step on the journey for me, the next step toward a greater sense of home—beyond our limited dimension.

In the end, what *does* matter? As Frances said during her life on Earth: "In the search for understanding and awakening we are drawn to those teachings that convey the deepest wisdom with the greatest beauty."

Four Stories
of Co-Creation

CYNTHIA SPRING "Consciousness and The Sea"
REGINA OCHOA "The Leaf That Came to Life"
NAOMI ROSE "The Gift of the Breath"
FRANCES VAUGHAN "What Matters Now"

"Consciousness and the Sea"

by Cynthia Spring

Where does the sea end? One might say it ends at the shoreline, but which shoreline? The one on a pleasant, sunny day when baby waves lap onto the sand? Or on a terribly stormy day when roiling waves slap the sides of the cliffs? Which shoreline? When?

Where does the sea end? The waterlines may be found, but what about the sea's breezes, its breath? Does it end at the cliffs, or does it waft into the nearby fishing village, filling the air with the taste of salt and the smell of fish?

Where does the sea end? Its bounty is gathered every day. When a fish, or a wrap of seaweed finds its way to a plate hundreds of miles away. Is that the sea's way of getting around?

Where does the sea end? One might say, "After I leave the beach and go home." The sea harbors our unconscious. Humans arrived as sea creatures. We carry our sea birth in the salty waters that flow in our bodies. So where *does* the sea end?

We speak of forests as "a sea of green," and the night sky as "a sea of stars." Where do those seas end? Perhaps we carry those seas within us also. Perhaps there is nowhere we can make a cut between the stars and the forests and the sea and ourselves. Perhaps it is All One.

———————————

Cynthia Spring is the co-author of this book. For more about her, see *About the Authors* at the end of the book.

Illustration by Naomi Rose.

"A New Leaf"

by Regina Ochoa

When I write, I pause time. Time stops. The outside world stops. The zig and zag of life refrain in a holding pattern.

This morning I fetched what I thought to be a leaf and twig from the dog's water bowl outdoors. The leaf, chartreuse green and limp, weighed little in my hand.

Slowly it came to life, looking at me, then stretched itself out. One furled leg flicked a droplet of water as it unfolded a transparent lime green wing. Two bulging camouflaged eyes stared at me from its alien-shaped head. Then—its two front legs folded, touching its feet together—he dipped his head.

"Thank you." I heard, clear as the day.

"You're welcome," I answered aloud, without pause.

"I nearly drowned. I was going to let go when you plucked me from my death."

"I will set you on a stem of the lilac bush. Where you can safely sit to dry and wake from your near-final sleep."

I moved the praying mantis to the plant. Carefully, it grabbed the narrow stem with a jointed foot, wrapped its other three feet around the thin leafless wood, and flipped upside down, hanging on the lilac.

I watched this tiny piece of life balancing between worlds—mine, and its life and death.

Time stopped when I interacted with the tiny insect.

Moments earlier, time had nearly ended for the mantis. Yet, now, we are in the same instance, frequency—vibration. And somehow, communicating.

I have no issue talking with discarnate beings. Spirits come and go around here. They stop by for a chat, sharing a message for me to deliver. I often feel like a mail carrier, crossing back and forth between realms of physical to non-physical.

But this morning, I crossed a different barrier. One where I could hear from another species, listening to the intelligence of this life form.

Sure, I talk to the dogs all the time. I often speak aloud what I imagine their cartoon bubble drawn above their head might read: "Feed me. It's 4 o'clock," or, "I know you said, 'Walk.'" Or, "My foot has a sticker on it! Get it out!" And, "It's the FedEx truck coming! They have biscuits!"

We imagine talking scenarios with our pets because of the bond we create with them. They are part of the family, learning from us and how to understand us. Our pets are amazing creatures. I know we communicate with them. So often, we have no idea we have given them signals they can read, but we are oblivious to our tell-tale actions.

But this morning's intercourse with the praying mantis was different. The insect's voice was instant, a recognizable thought response to my actions. I felt it. The mantis' appreciation was palatable.

This interaction between a summertime bug and myself opened another channel for me to tune into and listen to.

Through the action of saving the bright green insect, I experienced an immediate impact—an unexpected response. All from the praying mantis, the water droplet it dispersed into the hot air, and all the moisture evaporating from the tiny creature as it sat drying on the lilac stem.

The floodgates holding back the realms of possibilities opened wide. It reminds me that every action on this earth creates an impression. The tiniest pebbles dropped into still water create ever-expanding ripples.

This mantis reminds me we are the water and the pebble. We are the silt beneath the water and its microcosm; we are the soil on the banks, the plants and animals, and the air we breathe. We are of identical organic make-up, just arranged differently.

We are all energy.

We are molecules moving about, atop, and through an energy-dense place: physical, mental, emotional, and spiritual collisions of creation.

We are conscious, sentient beings living among many other sentient life forms. And we are all connected.

Listen. You can hear the others.

This morning time stopped. It is a wake-up moment, a reminder of what I had forgotten.

Pause to listen. There are worlds of voices speaking to us.

Regina Ochoa, a clairvoyant medium and trance channel, has worked with invisible energies for more than sixty years, communicating with discarnate spirits and delivering messages to their surviving loved ones. Through her unique gift, Ochoa brings comfort and hope to many, with the knowledge that the mind, soul, and consciousness survive physical death. Regina was one of several psychics who were contacted by crew members of the Challenger rocket after it blew up and killed all seven of them in January of 1986. (The "Resources" section cites the website where you can read the transcript of the channeled material.)

Ochoa has participated with the Foundation for Mind Being Research, Palo Alto, CA (FMBR.org); The Challenger Crew Channeling, *https://challengercc.org*, *Channeling the Challenger Astronauts: 30-Year Afterlife Communication Project* with medium Jeanne Love; and The Columbia Crew Channeling, *https://challengercc.or/col-index.php*. Facebook: Cosmic Voices Network, *https://www.cosmicvoices.network*. Regina's website is: *https://www.reginaochoa.com*

Illustration by Annelisa Ochoa.

"The Gift of the Breath"

by Naomi Rose

The breath is a co-creation. I may unconsciously view it as "my" breath, but I do not create it. It is given to me, moment by moment, breath by breath. Through the breath, life itself is given to me, over and over. Will I realize this? Will I retain it? Or will I unremember this reality, letting it slip out with the exhale?

How remarkable it is, in the pull and press of what goes on inside the mind, to stop the chatter, even for a moment, and return attention to the breath. Uncomplaining, always there, it seems to wake up with a pleased little start, like a cat awakening from a snooze in the sun: "Oh," it seems to say, "you *noticed* me! You noticed that I am cooler on the inhale, warmer on the exhale; that your belly swells out gently as you breathe in, and contracts as you breathe out. Your noticing me brings me into fuller life. We are in this together."

Such a call to recognize the presence of Something beyond us, the breath. So close, so intimate, so ordinary, so forgettable. And yet when I remember—"Oh, I've been paying attention to the scampering, scattering movements of my mind, so focused on the worries of the future, the fraying blanket of the past—and yet here is this breath, *this* breath, alive and never-before breathed, and somehow available to my awareness in a relational, reciprocal way. Why had I not noticed this a moment ago? Why is it not the center of my awareness?" And in that moment, it is.

Breath, when I am present to it, *is* relational, reciprocal, co-creational. As I open to its presence and sense where it touches my body, that noticing itself expands the breath. Lightens it, makes it more subtle, a looser weave. And then surprising insights, even revelations may come—as if the breath went and fetched them from some higher realm and brought them down to my level, to raise me up. Sometimes, these revelations are so remarkable that I am lifted out of my usual small sense of "me," into something vast as the ocean, the sky. Sometimes—a few times, at least, years ago—the breath became so subtle that it brought me back the actual whiff of perfume. Amazed, delighted, I did not want to leave my bed while it lasted, lest in making a move I might lose it. Eventually it did pass, but to this day I retain the memory of its once having been given—a radiant, surprising, fragrant gift.

This breath—my breath, your breath—is a carrier between worlds, more patient than we realize. It waits for us to notice it: and then, once we do, it becomes at once both pliable to our attention and our teacher, opening us to the miracle of our being, of being alive, of becoming more than we thought possible. *This* breath, and now *this* breath, and now *this* one....

This breath, this friend, this link with what is invisible that we take into ourselves and it knows how to distribute itself throughout the innards of our being — our bloodstream, our bones, our organs, our cells — this breath can teach us, heal us, befriend us all the way to our very last.

And when that has come and gone, our last breath, what then? Perhaps we enter into those realms that the breath has hinted at during our attentiveness in life—those realms from which it has fetched the insights, revelations, innovations, fragrances that gave us the foretastes we experienced and treasured.

Be with your breath. Let it befriend you. Give your best attention to it. It will bring you treasures unimagined. It will bring you all the way home.

Naomi Rose is the editor of all three books by Cynthia Spring and Frances Vaughan in the Greater Reality Series (7 *Questions About Life After Death, 7 Questions About the Greater Reality*, and the current volume). The creator of the Writing from the Deeper Self approach, as a Book Developer and Creative Midwife she offers creative encouragement and professional guidance to people writing books about the inner life. She is the author of books on the creative process and other subjects, as well as an illustrator. Both the image illustrating this essay and the above essay by Cynthia Spring first appeared in *The Wave and The Drop: Wisdom Stories About Death and Afterlife*, by Cindy Spring (Wisdom Circles Publishing, 2018). Naomi's professional website is: *https//:www.naomirose.net*.

"What Matters Now?"

By Frances Vaughn

(Channeled by Regina Ochoa)

I cannot answer for anyone but myself. So I observe, listen, and see the light through all the darkness of the existing chaos.

Does history repeat itself? Maybe, but this time is different.

Why? Because we can make a difference. Our thoughts make a difference. Our intentions make a statement. How we proceed through each day, hour, and moment changes the outcome.

When stepping out of the scene, that chaos, there is more than one conception of life—a good deal more. In fact, it's infinite.

A universe is not only one but multiple, unlimited universes. The continuous expanse of our universe has no boundaries. Therefore, there are no barriers to stopping thought or intention.

So our reflections, our choices, reach into the infinite. Each dream becomes a ripple in space, expanding unlimited and influencing further.

The key is acknowledging there is an even greater, more significant concept to change than what humankind embraces.

How can we change ourselves to think, create, co-exist, and evolve into the larger consciousness of life? Life is more than a human form or a Universe. Life is energy.

I hear your fear.

You ask, "I understand we are just a cog in the wheel. But we are a broken cog! So how do we fix the wheel—our Earth?"

With the intention of kindness. With compassion, with respect—no judgment.

Allow harmony to be a guiding star, a North Star to focus the intention to heal.

The fear that we don't matter is the obstacle to accepting our purpose—the fear we can't do anything to change an outcome.

However, change comes with small movements yet lasting ones.

Replace fear with trust—your actions do make a difference. Our words, our thoughts, and our intentions do matter.

As in the story of the drowning praying mantis, its life mattered. An action to remove it from the water mattered. Interaction between species is the illustration of co-existence. There was compassion and gratefulness.

One moment brought balance and then allowed life to flow forward. As a result, both species benefit from the other's existence.

What matters now?

Live your life knowing you are important, your thoughts and ideas make a difference, and your words and actions have weight.

Everything we think has a direct consequence on the flow of life.

We change the outcome by making our thoughts count.

Our intentions matter.

You matter.

Frances Vaughan is the co-creator of this book, along with the other two books in the Greater Reality series. The essay was channeled by Regina Ochoa for this book.

Sources and Endnotes

Story 1

Source of Story 1

This is historical fiction. The details about the Benedictine monastery are all true. The character and the event are fiction. Material for this story was drawn from *To Pause At the Threshold* by Esther de Waal, and from *The Rule of Benedict: A Spirituality for the 21st Century* by Joan Chittister. (*See* "Resources" section for full information on books.)

Endnotes

Frances: *It is a gathering of friends, as we used to do as a sixsome.* This refers to the frequent meetings during Frances' lifetime of Frances and her husband, Cynthia Spring and her husband, and another couple.

Eric Garner was a young man in New York City who was killed by a policeman. His mother now makes appearances on behalf of mothers who have lost their children through violence with police.

Esther de Waal, *To Pause at the Threshold: Reflections on Living on the Border.* (New York: Church Publishing Inc., 2004, paraphrased from p. 57.)

Story 2

Source of Story 2

The Frank Callahan story is an abridgement of a channeled message given to medium Jeanne Love in 2006. (*See* "Resources" section for full message.)

Endnotes

Frances: *When a soul recognizes itself as I am the I AM, it becomes united with the All There Is.* (*See* Frances' poem, "*I Am the Air I Breathe....*" at the end of Story 2.)

STORY 3

Source of Story 3

"Harps in the Trees" was given to us by Cheryl Ann Fulton, a master performer and teacher of the harp. Her story of traveling to a Harp Festival in Edinburgh, Scotland with some of her students and then visiting the grove of trees from which the harps were produced that they were playing is true. (*See* "Resources" section for the documentary film of their trip and a list of Cheryl's CDs.)

Endnotes

Frances: *Right now during this pandemic on earth, so much is evolving through the heroic efforts of so many millions of people whose life trajectory brought them to this moment....*

"Right now" refers to 2023.

STORY 4

Source of Story 4

This story is a fictionalized composite from a collection of stories about parents who developed a communication channel with their sons or daughters who had died. Each detail in the story is a common occurrence in such communication.

Endnotes

The organization where parents gather in groups to share their stories about connecting with their children who have died is called The Big Circle. The website is https://welcometoeternity.com.

Cynthia: *So many teenagers are committing suicide.*

(*See* "Resources" section for article, "Hello from Heaven," and reference to the step-by-step guide on how to contact a loved one on the other side from Book Two, *Seven Questions about the Greater Reality*, by Cynthia Spring and Frances Vaughan.)

STORY 5

Source of Story 5

Dr. Jerry Abraham is a real person. Roy is a fictitious character created for this story. The details in this story were taken from two major news stories in which Dr. Abraham was featured. (*See* "Resources" section.)

STORY 6

Source of Story 6

The refugee camp Za'atari exists in Jordan near the Syrian border. The story of Ingrid and Hassan is a fiction. Cynthia was alerted to the story by a column in the *New York Times* written by Nicholas Kristof titled, "Starving Children Don't Cry." (*See* "Resources" section.)

STORY 7

Source of Story 7

This is a true story, written by Regina Ochoa, who describes the last hours of her friend Dana's life. Regina is a skilled medium and was able to help Dana make her death transition. Frances was also present, and participated in the passing.

REFERENCES

STORY 1

Books

Joan Chittister. *The Rule of Benedict: A Spirituality for the 21st Century*. Chestnut Ridge, NY: Crossroad Publishing, 2010.

Esther de Waal. *To Pause at the Threshold: Reflections on Living on the Border*. New York: Church Publishing Inc., 2004.

STORY 2

Channeled messages

Frank Callahan's story appears in full on the "Cosmic Voices" website: *https://cosmicvoices.network*

STORY 3

Videos on the Harp Festival in Scotland

14-minute documentary of the trip to the Harp Festival in Scotland: *https://www.youtube.com/watch?v=078IGSP9Cy0*

Music video, "Chant for the Trees" (excerpted from the above documentary): *https://youtu.be/X70GkDbyzQ4*

Audios of harp music

Cheryl Ann Fulton's harp music, along with her group, is available under *Angelorum—The Harps in the Trees* on: magnatune, Pandora, Spotify, Amazon Music, and iTunes.

STORY 4

Books

Bill and Judy Guggenheim, *Hello from Heaven: A New Field of Research-After-Death Communication Confirms That Life and Love Are Eternal*. NY: Penguin Random House, 1997.

Laura Lynne Jackson, *The Light Between Us: Lessons for the Living*. New York: Dial Press, 2016.

Cynthia Spring and Frances Vaughan, *Seven Questions about the Greater Reality*. Book Two in The Greater Reality series. El Cerrito, CA: Wisdom Circles Publishing, 2020. (Includes a step-by-step guide on how to contact someone "on the other side," p. 159.)

Organizations
The Big Circle: https://welcometoeternity.com/

Statistics
Sandy Cohen, "Suicide Rate Highest Among Teens and Young Adults," *UCLA Health* (March 15, 2022), https://connect.uclahealth.org/2022/03/15/suicide-rate-highest-among-teens-and-young-adults/

"Youth Suicide Statistics," http://prp.jasonfoundation.com/facts/youth-suicide-statistics/

STORY 5

News stories
Dr. Jerry Abraham was featured in two major news stories:

Los Angeles Times article: https://www.latimes.com/california/story/2021-01-29/coronavirus-covid-vaccine-equity-hospital-south-los-angeles-kedren-health

On the Rachel Maddow show: https://www.msnbc.com/rachel-maddow/watch/removing-barriers-is-key-to-getting-vaccine-to-underserved-communities-100619845748

STORY 6

Articles on refugee camps
"Inside the World's Five Largest Refugee Camps," UNHCR (The UN Refugee Agency): https://www.unrefugees.org/news/inside-the-world-s-five-largest-refugee-camps/

Videos on refugee camps
"Step into a Refugee Camp," *New York Times* (Jordan Refugee Camp): https://www.nytimes.com/video/world/middleeast/00000004844523/who-are-the-syrian-refugees.html

Additional Resources

Films

Daniel Drasin, *Calling Earth*: *https://vimeo.com/101171248*. A five-minute preview is available at *https://vimeo.com/184237981*.

This remarkable 95-minute feature documentary introduces us to communication with the other side via electronic devices (recorders, telephones, TVs, computers, etc.) This phenomenon, known as Instrumental trans-Communication (ITC), has been well documented at least since the 1950s and provides robust objective evidence for an afterlife.

Books

Esther de Waal, *To Pause at the Threshold: Reflections on Living on the Border.* NY: Church Publishing Inc., 2004.

Dan Drasin. *A New Science of the Afterlife: Space, Time and the Consciousness Code.* NY: Simon & Schuster, 2023.

Arthur Hastings. *With the Tongues of Men and Angels: A Study of Channeling.* NY: Holt, Reinhart and Winston, 1991.

Jon Klimo. *Channeling: Investigations on Receiving Information from Paranormal Sources.* Berkeley, CA: North Atlantic Books, 1998.

Raymond Moody, Jr., M.D. *Life After Life.* New York: Bantam Books, 1975.

Jane Roberts/Seth. *The Nature of Personal Reality.* San Rafael, CA: Amber-Allen, reprinted 1994.

Websites

For the Challenger Crew Channeling, go to:
- https://challengercc.org, *Channeling the Challenger Astronauts: 30-Year Afterlife Communication Project*
- The Columbia Crew Channeling, *https://challengercc.or/col-index.php.*
- Cosmic Voices Network, *https://www.cosmicvoices.network.*

Dan Drasin: *https://www.dandrasin.com/*

Regina Ochoa: *https://www.reginaochoa.com*

Cindy Spring: *https://cindyspring.com*

Frances Vaughan interview on "Spirituality and Psychology" with Jeffrey Mishlove of "Thinking Allowed": *https://www.youtube. com/watch?v=61UxnP2y9II*

For more resources
Cynthia Spring and Frances Vaughan, *Seven Questions About Life After Life:* Book One in the Greater Reality Series. El Cerrito, CA: Wisdom Circles Publishing, 2019.

Cynthia Spring and Frances Vaughan, *Seven Questions About the Greater Reality:* Book Two in the Greater Reality Series. El Cerrito, CA: Wisdom Circles Publishing, 2020.

ACKNOWLEDGMENTS

Seven Stories to Light the Way Home is the third volume of a trilogy begun by Frances Vaughan and Cynthia Spring in early 2018 and completed in the spring of 2023. The co-creation was mainly the work of four individuals in the early days (Frances, Cynthia, Naomi Rose as excellent editor and packager, and Margaret Copeland as superb book designer). I'm blessed to have such multi-talented collaborators. That team was augmented by Regina Ochoa for Book 3. You will see Regina's magnificent work in the seventh story, *Time to Go Home*, as well as her essay, *A New Leaf*. Regina became involved in many aspects of production.

Along the way, medium Jeanne Love and world-class harpist Cheryl Ann Fulton made generous contributions of their stories. Reviewers Shelli Fried, Patti Hamel, and Judith Frank gave us needed feedback.

Charles Garfield, Cynthia's husband, was indispensable in the roles of editor, critic, cheerleader, and inspiration to stay the course. Charlie and Frances were close friends during her incarnation. Author, producer, and all-around chronicler of the greater reality Dan Drasin gave us much help and important connections when we needed them.

A special tribute to my brother Mark and his partner, Jane, for allowing me to share the last months of his life, so that a book on passage to the afterlife is not just a concept but a day-to-day experience with all its intense pain and depths of emotion.

To Susan Halpern, whose testimonial became the perfect gift at the right time.

To Topanga Home Grown, the West Coast gift shop where one will be able to find the "Greater Reality series" well stocked.

Of course no book succeeds without the unnamed printers, bookstore employees, wholesalers, and word of mouth from friends of the authors. One book component often overlooked is the obvious one: readers. They read the books, but they also sent ahead their wishes for the kind of book they need for their journey at this point. Thank you. We hope we helped.

Frances and I want to make one more acknowledgment: each other. I remember walking down a street together and saying to Frances: "I'd love to do a book together." We did. Three!

Participating in a Wisdom Circle

If you are inspired to explore the questions raised in the Greater Reality book series, including this one as well as Book One, *Seven Questions About the Afterlife*, and Book Two, *Seven Questions About the Greater Reality*—to see what can be learned from the "other side" ("the balcony," as Frances Vaughan calls it) and how that can be applied to our lives on *this* side (both individually and as a global community), then you might want to form / participate in a "Wisdom Circle."

Developed by Cynthia Spring along with Charles Garfield and Sedonia Cahill in their book, *Wisdom Circles: A Guide to Self-Discovery and Community Building in Small Groups*, Wisdom Circles are defined as "places to practice heart-to-heart communication skills, to heal wounds, to find the courage to act upon that 'still small voice within.' Places to share a vision, define a mission. Places where we can create a community, where we can learn to be more fully ourselves, while simultaneously becoming an integral part of the group."

The book shows how to form your own Wisdom Circles with friends and community members, based on ten simple guidelines. It is a handbook for creating compassionate community for the twenty-first century.

The many purposes served by a Wisdom Circle include a place to:

- Create a safe container for full participation
- Practice communication skills (e.g., listening from the heart, speaking from direct experience, making room for silence to enter, express gratitude)
- Heal wounds
- Find the courage to act upon that small voice within.

- Share a vision or define a mission
- Explore a question affecting both individuals and the global community

"In Wisdom Circles, the authors remind us that we are all healers and invite us to once again reclaim the healing power of a simple and genuine connection with one another. Showing us that listening is the most effective tool of healing, the authors offer a step-by-step manual for using the power of community to clarify our authentic values and recover our deepest sense of meaning." —RACHEL NAOMI REMEN, M.D., *author of* Kitchen Table Wisdom: Stories That Heal

"We have used wisdom circles extensively at our annual conferences and in our community groups. Over and over again, participants find in these circles greater self-awareness and deeper communication with one another. Remarkably, this requires no particular magic other than the magic that arises out of respectful contact with each other and our own direct experience. This book will help you create a context of trust, belonging, and common purpose so you can experience that magic yourself." —THOMAS J. HURLEY, *Director of Education, Institute of Noetic Sciences*

You can buy a reissued copy of *Wisdom Circles* from your local bookstore or an online retailer (such as Amazon, Barnes & Noble, Bookshop, etc.).

Wisdom Circles: A Guide to Self-Discovery and Community Building in Small Groups. Charles Garfield, Cindy Spring, and Sedonia Cahill. Originally published by Hyperion, 1998. Republished by The Apocryphile Press, 2021. The website is: *www.wisdom-circles.org*

About the Authors

 **Frances Vaughan** was a psychologist and teacher who inspired everyone she met to be his or her higher self. She wrote books and papers that carried on the wisdom and compassion that she gathered from many lifetimes. She served as a trustee for 19 years at the Fetzer Institute, which helps build a spiritual foundation for a loving world. As a transpersonal psychotherapist, she helped guide her clients to find the source of their healing. She continues her work through this book collaboration.

> *"Frances was a respected 'Wise Woman' and a true elder. She embodied the strong feminine and was a model of extraordinarily bright mind meeting an ever-expanding heart."* —FRANK OSTESESKI, *Founder of Metta Institute, author of* The Five Invitations: Discovering What Death Can Teach Us About Living Fully.

Books: *Awakening Intuition* (Anchor Books, 1979); *The Inward Arc: Healing in Psychotherapy and Spirituality* (iUniverse, 2001); and *Shadows of the Sacred: Seeing Through Spiritual Illusions* (Quest Books, 1995). With her husband, Roger Walsh, she was co-editor of *Paths Beyond Ego: The Transpersonal Vision* (Tarcher, 1993), and *Gifts from A Course in Miracles*, including *Accept this Gift, A Gift of Peace* and *A Gift of Healing* (Tarcher, 1995), published separately and as one volume.

Cynthia Spring is an author, social activist, and explorer of the unconventional. Since the mid 1990s, she has been active in local ecology in the San Francisco area. She co-founded two ecology nonprofits, EarthTeam and Close to Home, as well as serving as coordinator for Earth Day 2000 for the Bay Area. Her explorations have been in the fields of spirituality, transpersonal psychology, and personal growth. She lives in Northern California with her husband, Charlie.

Books: *Seven Questions About Life After Life,* in collaboration with Frances Vaughan (Book 1 in "The Greater Reality" series, Wisdom Circles Publishing, 2019); *Seven Questions About the Greater Reality,* in collaboration with Frances Vaughan (Book 2 in "The Greater Reality" series, Wisdom Circles Publishing, 2020); *The Wave and The Drop: Wisdom Stories about Death and Afterlife* (Wisdom Circles Publishing, 2018), and *Wisdom Circles: A Guide to Self-Discovery and Community Building in Small Groups* (Hyperion, 1998 / The Apocryphile Press, 2021). She co-authored *Sometimes My Heart Goes Numb: Love and Caregiving in a Time of AIDS* with Charles Garfield (Jossey-Bass, 1995). She co-edited the anthology *Earthlight: Spiritual Wisdom for an Ecological Age* (2007). She was also the producer (1981-1996) of over 100 nonfiction audiobooks. See *https://cindyspring.com*

Additional Books by Cynthia Spring

Seven Questions About Life After Life: Book One in the Greater Reality Series. Cynthia Spring and Frances Vaughan. El Cerrito, CA: Wisdom Circles Publishing, 2019.

Seven Questions About the Greater Reality: Book Two in the Greater Reality Series. Cynthia Spring and Frances Vaughan. El Cerrito, CA: Wisdom Circles Publishing, 2020.

The Wave and The Drop: Wisdom Stories About Death and Afterlife. Cindy Spring. Foreword by Dr. Charles Garfield. El Cerrito, CA: Wisdom Circles Publishing, 2018.

Wisdom Circles: A Guide to Self-Discovery and Community Building in Small Groups. Charles Garfield, Cindy Spring, and Sedonia Cahill. Originally published by Hyperion, 1998. Republished by The Apocryphile Press, 2021.

Sometimes My Heart Goes Numb: Love and Caregiving in a Time of AIDS. Charles Garfield and Cindy Spring. San Francisco: Jossey-Bass, 1995.

Earthlight: Spiritual Wisdom for an Ecological Age. Cindy Spring and Anthony Manousos, editors. Friends Bulletin, 2007.

CPSIA information can be obtained
at www.ICGtesting.com
Printed in the USA
JSHW020308260623
43762JS00005B/25